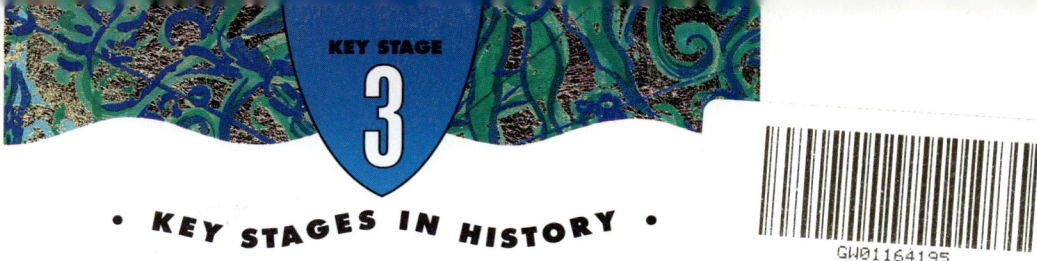

KEY STAGES IN HISTORY

THE MAKING OF THE UNITED KINGDOM

L E Snellgrove

Nelson

Thomas Nelson and Sons Ltd
Nelson House   Mayfield Road
Walton-on-Thames   Surrey
KT12 5PL   UK

51 York Place
Edinburgh
EH1 3JD   UK

Thomas Nelson (Hong Kong) Ltd
Toppan Building 10/F
22A Westlands Road
Quarry Bay   Hong Kong

Thomas Nelson Australia
102 Dodds Street
South Melbourne
Victoria 3205   Australia

Nelson Canada
1120 Birchmount Road
Scarborough   Ontario
M1K 5G4   Canada

© L E Snellgrove 1992

First published by Thomas Nelson and Sons Ltd 1992

ISBN 0-17-435058-9
NPN 9 8 7 6 5 4 3 2 1

All rights reserved. No paragraph of this publication may be reproduced, copied or transmitted save with written permission or in accordance with the provisions of the Copyright, Design and Patents Act 1988, or under the terms of any licence permitting limited copying issued by the Copyright Licensing Agency, 90 Tottenham Court Road, London W1P 9HE.

Any person who does any unauthorised act in relation to this publication may be liable to criminal prosecution and civil claims for damages.

Printed in Hong Kong.

The author and publishers are grateful to the following for permission to reproduce copyright materials:

Ancient Art and Architecture Collection: pages 74, 77;
Architectural Review: page 14;
Archiv fur Kunst und Geschichte, Berlin: page 38 (Sherbourne Castle, Dorset);
Bridgeman Art Library: pages 20 (Weston Park, Shropshire), 21 (Bible Society, London), 24 (*centre left*) (Kunsthistorisches Museum, Vienna), (*far let*) (Belvoir Castle, Leicestershire), (*below left*) (Louvre, Paris), 28, 35, 36, 49 (Roy Miles Fine Paintings, London), 63 (Burghley House, Stamford, Lincolnshire), 65 (*below*) (House of Lords), 68, 95 (Institute of Directors, London), 96 (Historical Portraits Ltd, London), 97 (House of Commons), 98 (King Street Galleries, London);
Trustees of the British Museum: page 43 (*left*), 81, 83 (*left*);
British Library: page 85 (*below*);
Cambridge University Collection: pages 6, 71 (*below*);
Duke of Beccleuch and Queensberry: page 24 (*top left*);
The College of Arms: page 18;
Earl of Leicester, Holkham Hall, Coke Estates Ltd: page 7;
The Edinburgh Photographic Library: page 87 (Peter Davenport);
e.t. archive (Marquess of Bath, Longleat), 55 (*above*) (National Maritime Museum), 100;
Mary Evans Picture Library: pages 11, 19, 45, 65 (*above*), 83 (*right*), 107 (*below*);
Fotomas Index: pages 42, 46, 50, 57, 61, 62;
Michael Holford: pages 22, 73 (above right), 106 (below);
House ot Lords Record Office: page 94 (reproduced by courtesy of the Clerk of the Records);
Hulton-Deutsch Collection: pages 55 (below), 88;
A F Kersting: pages 16, 39 (*right*), 40, 43 (*right*), 104;
Louth Grammar School: page 44 (drawing courtesy of Ladybird Books);
Mansell Collection: pages 30, 32, 40 (*above and below*), 67, 71 (*above*), 78, 85 (*above*), 107 (*above*), 109;
Bill Meadows Picture Library: pages 9 (right), 58;
Mitchell Library, Glasgow: page 93;
National Library of Scotland: page 99;
National Maritime Museum: page 23;
National Portrait Gallery: pages 12, 19, 24 (above right), (*below right*), 53, 70, 73 (*below right*), 75, 82, 89, 92;
National Trust Photographic Library: pages 33 (Hawkley Studios), 39 (*left*) (John Bethell);
Peter Newark's Historical Pictures: pages 34, 64;
Norfolk Museums Service: page 27;
Popperfoto: page 91;
Ann Ronan Picture Library: page 73 (*above left*);
The Royal Collection: pages 17, 24 (*centre right*);
Edwin Smith: page 9 (*left*);
Tate Gallery: page 106 (*above*);
Weidenfeld Archives: page 56;
Woburn Abbey Collection: page 29 (reproduced with the kind permission of the Marquess of Tavistock and the Trustees of the Bedford Estate.)

The engraving of Dyrham Park on page 102 comes from *The Ancient and Present State of Gloucestershire*, by R Atkyns, published in 1712.

Preface

To make this book both interesting and accessible to twelve- and thirteen- year olds, great care has been taken to use clear, straightforward language. To allow adequate scope for explaining ideas and concepts, the basic text has been given a more generous allocation of space than is commonly found at this level. Experience of young readers suggests that extreme brevity rarely aids understanding or stimulates enduring interest.

The selection of material has been determined by the relevant core study unit of the National Curriculum. Most of the prescribed topics have been incorporated into chapters with a chronological structure. This allows for the integration of social and economic with political history and gives the reader a framework for developing some sense of time. For ease of reference, all the topics in the Orders are highlighted in bold type in the *Index*.

Sources – both written and pictorial – are numbered consecutively in each chapter. Not all are keyed into the text, to make the book easier to read. There are textual references to all written sources, but only to those picture sources which directly support the narrative. All documentary extracts are provided with brief introductions to set them in context and have been carefully edited and glossed; they have not been paraphrased because this would destroy their 'period flavour'. In this respect, the complexity and tortuous structure of much sixteenth and seventeenth-century prose presented a particular problem, but one which has been solved, I hope, with the least possible alteration to the originals.

The *Assessment Tasks* at the end of each chapter cover all three Attainment Targets in a structured and balanced way, taking account of the double weighting of AT1. The additional groups of questions in the body of the text are designed to stimulate both general discussion and clarification of historical terms and references. Many are also relevant to the Statements of Attainment.

I should like to thank my wife, Jean, and my collaborator, R.J. Cootes, for their encouragement, help and advice.

L.E. Snellgrove

Contents

1 THE TUDOR REALM
England in the early sixteenth century

Farming and the countryside	6
Estates and degrees	7
North and South	9
Towns and cities	10
The monarchy	12
Crown and Parliament	13
Assessment tasks	15

2 THE WELSH PRINCE
Henry VIII, Reformation and Union with Wales

Defender of the Faith	17
The King's Great Matter	18
The Reformation Parliament	19
Dissolution of the monasteries	20
The Pilgrimage of Grace	22
Welsh Acts of Union	23
Assessment tasks	26

3 CHURCH AND STATE
Elizabeth I, religion and Parliament

Protestant reforms	27
Mary – the Catholic Queen	28
The Elizabethan Church	30
The Society of Jesus	31
Elizabeth and her parliaments	31
Quarrel with Spain	33
Assessment tasks	37

4 GLORIANA'S PEOPLE
Elizabethan life

Mansions, manor houses and cottages	39
'Keep some great man as a friend'	40
Poor Laws	41
Schools and universities	42
The theatre	45
Plantations in Ireland	47
Assessment tasks	48

5 THE ROAD TO CIVIL WAR
James I, Charles I and 'Divine Right'

'No bishop, no king'	50
The Gunpowder Plot	51
The Petition of Right	53
Eleven Years' Tyranny	54
National Covenant	56
Grand Remonstrance and War	57
Assessment tasks	59

6 DIVIDED BY THE SWORD
Civil War and the rule of Cromwell

Cavaliers and Roundheads	60
From Edgehill to Nantwich	61
Marston Moor	63
The New Model Army	63
Trial and execution	65
Commonwealth and Protectorate	66
The Restoration, 1660	67
Assessment tasks	69

7 IDEAS AND DISCOVERIES

Arts and sciences in the seventeenth century

The world of Samuel Pepys	70
The Royal Society	72
Milton and Dryden	72
The Starry Messenger	74
Newton and gravity	75
Medicine and magic	76
The circulation of the blood	77
Assessment tasks	79

8 'THE GLORIOUS REVOLUTION'

James II overthrown

Tories and Whigs	80
The warming-pan baby	82
The fall of James II	83
The 1689 Settlement	84
Scotland – the massacre at Glencoe	86
'King Billy' in Ireland	87
Assessment tasks	90

9 BRITAIN UNITED

Crown, Parliament and Union with Scotland

Scotland – the poor relation	92
Act of Union, 1707	93
George of Hanover	94
The power of Parliament	96
The '15 and '45 rebellions	98
The last battle on British soil	99
Assessment tasks	101

10 A BRITISH EMPIRE

Britain in the early eighteenth century

Estates, degrees and 'the miserable'	103
The 'new look' North	105
London life	107
Colonies and trade	108
Britain and the New World	109
Assessment tasks	111
Index	112

1 The Tudor Realm

England in the early sixteenth century

THE TUDORS
Henry VII   1485-1509
Henry VIII   1509-1547
Edward VI   1547-1553
Mary   1553-1558
Elizabeth I 1558-1603

What was sixteenth-century England like, and how was it different from today? To answer this question we turn to the writings of the time. In 1505 King Henry VII asked Polydore Vergil to write a history of England. Polydore was an Italian scholar who spent many years in England. Much of his book tells of the doings of kings and noblemen. But he also wrote about the England he knew. We call this 'Tudor England' after the royal family who ruled from 1485 until 1603.

SOURCE 1

Polydore Vergil (1470–1555) here describes the England of his time. He was a churchman who came to live in England in 1502.

The whole country of Britain – which is called England and Scotland – is divided into four parts … One is inhabited by Englishmen, the other by Scots, the third of Welshmen, the fourth the Cornish people … All [are] different from each other, either in language, in customs, or else in laws … England, being the greatest part, is divided into 39 shires (counties) … The land is most fertile on this (the south) side of the Humber, for on the other side there are mountains … It has pretty valleys where are the houses of nobles and little towns because the people do not like cities.

Farming and the countryside

One thing mentioned by Polydore has not changed. The country divides naturally into two: the hills and mountains of the north and west, and the flatter lands of the south and east (**Source 1**). This affects farming; it is easier to grow crops in flat country and to keep cattle and sheep on hillsides. You are still more likely to see fields of corn south of the river Humber and flocks of sheep and cattle to the north and west.

The countryside looked different in the sixteenth century, especially in the south. Today it is parcelled into neat fields, fenced in by walls or hedges. In Tudor times it was mostly open and unfenced, with farmers working their individual strips rather like modern allotments (**Source 2**). Under this 'open field' system of farming, arable (ploughed) land for growing crops was divided into three large fields in each village. One field was left fallow (unused) each year to allow the goodness to return to the soil. Rougher, less suitable land was used to keep cattle, pigs or chickens. Because all the villagers

SOURCE 2

These fields around the village of Laxton in Nottinghamshire are still farmed on the open-field system.

The Tudor Realm

shared such land it was called the commons.

Fencing of fields is called enclosure. In Polydore's time, some landowners fenced their fields to grow better crops. More often enclosure was for sheep-farming. Looking after sheep requires fewer workers than arable farming so enclosure often threw people out of work. When this happened, the landowner would tell the villagers to pull down their houses and leave. Aerial photographs show us the outlines of many such 'lost' villages.

Enclosure of arable land meant more efficient farming and so more food to feed the growing population. Enclosure for sheep-runs increased the amount of wool English merchants could sell. But it led to distress and discontent in the countryside and this displeased the government. They did not want homeless, starving beggars roaming the countryside.

In Tudor times there were far fewer jobs, trades and professions than now. Most men and women lived and worked on the land. Even so, growing food was only part of a farmer's life. 'Do-it-yourself' work was essential – not a hobby as it is today. With few shops to sell ready-made goods, a farmer built his own house and made his own tools and furniture. His wife baked bread, brewed beer, spun wool, made clothes and turned milk into butter and cheese.

In such a world people could not afford to be wasteful. Flax was turned into linen to make towels, sheets and clothes. Poultry feathers made a mattress; cinders a path across a muddy farmyard. The blood and bones left over from animals killed for meat was used as manure. Acorns fed pigs, animal hide made leather drinking vessels, wayside herbs and flowers made medicines.

Estates and degrees

To own land was a sign of wealth and importance in society. Land was the basis of what Tudor people called your 'degree' or 'estate' – nowadays we would call it your 'class'. Owning a lot of land made a man a 'gentleman'. Those with no land at all were looked down upon as being of the lowest 'estate' **(Source 4)**.

Ownership of land gave a man the right to control the lives of others. The richest gentlemen held the most important jobs in the county, such as deputy lord-lieutenant (in charge of defence), justice of the peace or member of Parliament (MP). A gentleman's income was made up of rent paid by tenants for farming his fields, sales of timber from his woods and, in many cases, profits from mining on his land.

A gentleman was expected to show off his wealth. He built a fine mansion and filled it with paintings, expensive furniture and furnishings. He dined off gold and silver plates, drank from fine glassware and

SOURCE 3

Farming scenes from around the year 1500. At the bottom we see a man ploughing and, behind him, another dragging a harrow to break up the soil. Other workers are cutting wood. In the background, a man and woman are beating iron drums to imitate thunder and bring down a swarm of bees to their hives.

England in the early sixteenth century **7**

and wore costly clothes, some studded with precious stones. He wanted people in the future to know how rich and important he had been. So he had portraits painted (**Source 5**) and arranged to be buried in a grand tomb when he died.

Less wealthy gentlemen, of what was called 'the middling sort', held offices such as sheriff or mayor of a town. Such men copied their richer neighbours by improving their houses and furnishings. Yeomen, owning smaller amounts of land, were on the borderline of the gentleman class. They usually had between 20 and 40 hectares. Gentlemen at all levels did well during Tudor times. At the start they owned 40 per cent of the land of England, and at the end 60–70 per cent.

Those who owned little or no land – the 'common people' – had to work for wages. They were, as one gentleman put it, 'to be ruled, not to rule others'. This applied to any wage-earner, from the humble labourer to the highly-skilled craftsman. There were, however, some differences of rank among wage-earners. Labourers who had yearly contracts with their employers were better thought of than those hired by the day. Day-labourers often had to move from place to place to find work. They were sometimes thought to be beggars and arrested by the local sheriff.

SOURCE 4

William Harrison (1534–93) was a clergyman who spent many years writing his *Description of Britain*, from which this extract comes.

We in England divide our people into four sorts, as gentlemen, citizens or burgesses, yeomen, and artificers (craftsmen) and labourers. Of gentlemen, the first and chief, next the king, be dukes, marquesses, earls, viscounts and barons ... these are gentlemen of the greater sort, or lords and noblemen. The next unto them be knights, esquires and, last of all, they that simply be called gentlemen ... Citizens and burgesses be those that are free within cities ... Yeomen are freemen born English, who may dispose (sell) their own land ... The fourth and last people in England are day labourers, poor husbandmen (farmers) and all artificers, such as tailors, shoemakers, carpenters, brickmakers, [stone]masons etc.

SOURCE 5

Lord Cobham and his family, painted in 1567. Notice that the children are dressed like adults.

The Tudor Realm

SOURCE 6
The interior of Compton Wynyates Hall – an early Tudor mansion in Warwickshire.

SOURCE 7
Alnwick Castle, home of the Earls of Northumberland.

North and South

Polydore Vergil's division of the country into the flatter, more fertile south and the hilly north was more than just geographical. It also marked differences in wealth and ways of living. Southern England, especially around London, was dotted with prosperous ports, towns and villages. Its flat lands yielded rich crops. Easy trade routes to the Continent brought wealth to many merchant families. It was here that the richest gentlemen lived, in their fine mansions. It was here, also, that the government and the royal court were based. Few Tudor monarchs ever visited the north of their kingdom.

To travel north in those days was to enter another world. There were far fewer busy towns or crowded villages, and often only isolated farmhouses for miles on end. Rich soil gave way to the harder, stony ground of hills and mountains. Some areas had profitable industries, particularly woollen cloth-making in Yorkshire and coal-mining in Northumberland and Durham. Elsewhere farming folk were more likely to keep sheep and cattle than grow crops.

The hard, rugged life of the North produced tough soldiers who defended the Border against raids from the Scots. These

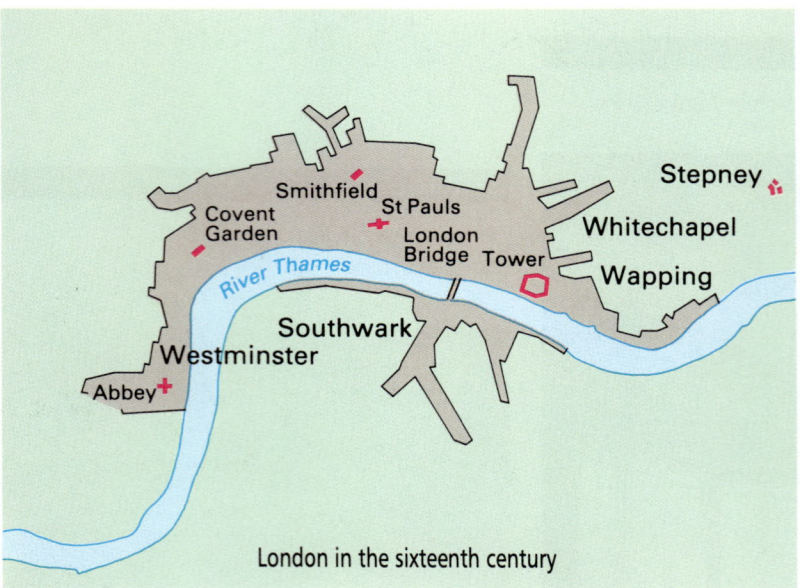

London in the sixteenth century

Towns and cities

The total population of England and Wales in 1500 was no more than 3 million – compared with 50 million today. England was greener then, with larger areas of forest and marshland. Roads were often little more than mud tracks. Towns were very small by modern standards. London, the largest, had about 60,000 inhabitants in 1500. Other important towns included Norwich (12,000 people), Bristol (10,000), Newcastle (10,000) and York (7,500). The chief industries were coal, tin and iron mining. In those days mines were usually in the country, on a landowner's estate. Industrial and factory towns as we know them did not exist.

Some towns were called boroughs. This meant they had been given the right to rule themselves by royal charter. Boroughs greatly valued their privileges and their officials, such as the mayor and aldermen (elder-men), took their jobs seriously. The mayor was elected by the craft and merchant guilds of the borough. It was his job to make sure that the town was well run. He had to see that it was kept as clean as possible (**Source 8**) and that shopkeepers who sold bad food or shoddy goods were punished.

London, the capital city, stood on the north bank of the river Thames. The river was used as a highway by Londoners to escape the narrow, crowded streets. Its waters were packed with boats of all shapes and sizes. London's position gave it many advantages (**Source 9**). It was hard for an enemy to attack, yet well placed for trade with the Continent and the wealthier parts of England. London was visited by many foreigners (**Source 10**) so its citizens knew more about the outside world than other English people.

During the Tudor century London's population increased rapidly, to around 200,000 by 1600. In the process, London swallowed up surrounding villages such as Whitechapel, Stepney and Wapping. The change was not always for the better. John Stow (see Source 9) grumbled that where

men looked upon local nobles such as the earls of Northumberland and Westmorland as their kings. It was said of Northumberland's men that they 'knew no prince but a Percy' – the Earl's family name. Such people paid little attention to a government which was two or three weeks' journey away.

A northern noble or gentleman was normally much poorer than his like in the South. The Earl of Northumberland, who lived in a castle and could call on a large force of fighting men, got £79 a year rent from his biggest estate at Alnwick. The Earl of Bedford, who lived not far from London and had no soldiers to call on, owned property worth £1496 a year.

SOURCE 8

These rules and regulations from Chelmsford in Essex (1564) are typical of those laid down by boroughs in the sixteenth century.

First, it is ordered that every inhabitant of the town shall scour and make clean the common gutter coming through the town, once in every month. Under pain of 12 pence fine ... Neither the butcher nor any person at any time hereafter shall throw horns, bones or any other filth in the street or in the river there, penalty 3 shillings 4 pence ... No inhabitant of any house shall kill any cattle or make any slaughter within the house, to the hurt and annoyance of his neighbours, penalty 20 shillings (£1).

SOURCE 9

John Stow wrote a history of London in 1598. Here he explains some of the advantages of London's position.

The river Thames opens upon France and Flanders (now Belgium), our mightiest neighbours, to whose doings we ought to take special note; and this city stands in such a convenient distance from the sea, as it is near enough for news of those [foreign] princes, and for resistance against them, far enough away for any sudden dangers from them ... Neither should I forget to mention that no place is so plentifully watered with springs as London is.

SOURCE 11

This drawing shows London at the end of the sixteenth century. On the left is the old St Paul's Cathedral. It had lost its spire by then but was still taller than most cathedrals today. On the right is London Bridge, then the only bridge across the Thames. Its nineteen arches almost blocked the flow of water and its roadway was lined on each side with shops.

SOURCE 10

Visitors to London have left us their impressions of the English people. This is part of a report sent home by an ambassador from Venice at the beginning of the sixteenth century.

The English are great lovers of themselves and of everything belonging to them; they think that there are no other men than themselves, and no other world but England ... They are ... very quick at everything they apply their minds to; few, however, apart from the clergy, are keen on the study of books ... They have a very high reputation as soldiers; and from the great fear the French have of them, one must believe this to be well deserved ... They are lacking affection to their children who, at the age of seven or nine years, they put out to hard service in the houses of other people.

QUESTIONS

1. Can you work out from Source 8 how people disposed of household rubbish in Tudor times? What difficulties could this cause?
2. Why did John Stow (Source 9) consider London to be at a 'convenient' distance from the sea?
3. Why would John Stow have thought it important to mention London's many springs?
4. What do the buildings shown in Source 11 tell you about life in London in the sixteenth century?

England in the early sixteenth century

there had once been 'fair hedges and long rows of elms' there were now 'filthy cottages' and 'alleys of small tenements (dwellings)'.

The monarchy

At the head of the kingdom stood the monarch. The nobles and the people liked to have a strong ruler. They remembered that weak kings in the past had often faced riots or rebellions. In the fifteenth century there had been wars between the two royal families of Lancaster and York to decide who should be king. These were called the Wars of the Roses because Yorkist soldiers sometimes wore a white rose and Lancastrians a red rose. During these conflicts one king was murdered and another killed in battle. The wars ended when Henry Tudor, a Lancastrian, defeated and killed the Yorkist king, Richard III, in 1485.

Nobody wanted such troubles again, so Tudor governments taught people that rebellion was a sin against God. Special

SOURCE 12

This is part of a *Homily Against Disobedience and Wilful Rebellion*, issued in 1571 to be read in churches.

How horrible a sin against God and man rebellion is ... For he that rebels is guilty not of a single sin ... but of the whole puddle and sink of all sins against God and man, against his prince, his country, his countrymen, his parents, his children, his kinsfolk, his friends and against all men ... Read the histories of all nations; look at the chronicles of our own country ... ye shall find that God never let a rebellion against a natural and lawful prince prosper.

SOURCE 13

Part of a painting showing scenes from the royal court in Tudor times.

sermons about obedience (called homilies) were read out regularly during church services **(Source 12)**. There was good reason to fear rebellion because the country had neither a regular army nor a police force and it took time to call up the militia (part-time soldiers). Savage punishments were inflicted on those who dared to rebel.

The lords, ladies and government officials who made up the royal court enjoyed dancing, singing, acting and hunting. There was also a serious side to court life. Some male courtiers were the monarch's advisers and belonged to the Great Council of nobles and bishops which was consulted on important matters. In between meetings of the Council, the kingdom was governed by a smaller group of nobles, the Privy Council. These men carried out royal commands, wrote letters and other documents, and dealt with important legal cases. Senior government ministers today still belong to a Privy Council which acts in the monarch's name.

Crown and Parliament

The day to day running of the country could be left to members of the Privy Council. But when new laws and taxes were required the monarch usually called a meeting of Parliament. Since the thirteenth century it had been the custom in England to invite two knights (landowners) from each county and two burgesses (citizens) from each borough to the palace of Westminster to advise the king and his Council ('the Lords'). These representatives of the people were known as the Commons **(Source 14)**.

The Commons were supposed to be elected in the counties by those owning land worth at least 40 shillings (£2) a year. But contests were rare. Instead, the leading families of the county decided, with the agreement of the '40 shilling freeholders', who should be their MP **(Source 15)**. In a similar way, borough councils chose the burgesses who would represent them. The number of borough seats grew during Tudor times, from 296 to 462, as new borough charters were granted.

Monarchs rarely called Parliament unless they wanted to impose taxes or change the law. Today, taxes are paid regularly for all sorts of purposes. In Tudor times a king or queen could only tax for

SOURCE 14

Sir Thomas Smith was secretary to Queen Elizabeth I. Here, in a book published in 1565, he describes the powers of Parliament.

The most high and absolute power of the realm of England consists in Parliament. Parliament cancels old laws, makes new ones ... establishes forms of religion, alters weights and measures, decides the succession to the throne, raises taxes, gives free pardons, condemns or finds innocent those whom the prince will put to trial. Parliament represents the power of the whole realm ... for every Englishman is intended to be there present, either in person or by a representative ... And the consent of the Parliament is taken to be every man's consent.

SOURCE 15

Here John Kingsmill, sheriff of Hampshire, writes to Thomas Wriothesley concerning the election of members for the shire (county) in April 1539.

Truly the majority of the [men] of the shire were very glad to have you as knight (MP) and so they have chosen you ... Furthermore, it has pleased my Lord Privy Seal that I should be a burgess (MP) ... of some borough in some other shire where I am not sheriff ... If you think it good, you may also have John Dalle who is a goodwitted fellow and says he will follow your advice.

QUESTIONS

1. In Source 14, what does Sir Thomas Smith mean when he says that 'every Englishman' is intended to be present in Parliament?

2. How was the way of choosing MPs in Tudor times different from today's method?

3. Townspeople gained greater influence in Parliament during the sixteenth century. Can you explain how this came about?

4. How is the job of the Commons' Speaker today different from Tudor times?

some special reason. Monarchs were expected to govern the kingdom out of their own income from rents on royal lands, customs duties and other fees. Henry VII, who rarely needed money, called few parliaments. His son, Henry VIII, required Parliament to make important new laws. Later, Queen Elizabeth I asked for taxes to pay for a war with Spain.

Parliament could only meet when called by the monarch. The Commons spent most of the time in a separate room, discussing the government's plans. After each session their chairman, the Speaker, went to the king and Lords to give the Commons' opinions and also to present their *petitions* (requests) and complaints. By the end of the sixteenth century the Crown faced a Commons of wealthy men who had a lot of influence in the country. They were usually carefully picked to make sure of their loyalty, but this did not stop them speaking up when they thought something was wrong.

SOURCE 16

The old Palace of Westminster, the meeting place of Parliament in Tudor times. The building was burnt down in 1834 and replaced with the modern Houses of Parliament.

The Tudor Realm

Assessment tasks

A Knowledge and understanding

1. a Why was it so important to own land in this period?
   b Whereabouts in Britain was land most valuable, and why?

2. How did the changes mentioned in this chapter affect (a) rich people, (b) the poor, and (c) the way England was governed?

3. Make a list of ways in which life in London and other towns in the sixteenth century was (a) different from today, (b) similar to today.

B Sources and interpretations

4. Here two modern historians write about the effects of enclosure during this period.

   Landlords found it necessary to increase their incomes by various practices of which enclosure ... and the raising of rents ... were the most hated. Contemporaries (people living at the time) put it all down to greed and wickedness ... They painted a picture of vast areas stripped of their peasantry ... and exploited as sheep-runs by lords ... This picture continues to be accepted, though most of the bases for it (reasons for believing it) have disappeared ... Enclosure [was] often the work of small farmers and yeomen [and] designed for better farming.
   (G.R. Elton, 1955)

   Much enclosure was by 'agreement' between the freeholders of a village. It is difficult to avoid the suspicion that on occasion 'agreement' was extorted (forced) from the weak by the strong ... We must recall too the loss of the right to pick up timber, hunt animals etc. on the common lands – the total loss of which must have been very serious for [the poorest] families.
   (Christopher Hill, 1967)

   In what ways do these accounts differ, and how might such differences have arisen?

5. Compare Sources 4 and 10.
   a How useful are they in helping us to understand sixteenth-century England?
   b Present the information in Source 4 in the form of a chart or diagram showing the different levels of society.
   c Source 10 is written by a foreigner. Do you think this makes it more or less reliable?

6. What do Sources 14 and 15 tell you about people's attitudes towards Parliament in this period?

2 The Welsh Prince

Henry VIII, Reformation and Union with Wales

SOURCE 1

The tombs of King Henry VII (1485–1509) and his Queen, Elizabeth of York, in Westminster Abbey.

As night fell on 7 August 1485, a small force led by Henry Tudor landed at Dale, near Milford Haven in Wales. Henry was a Lancastrian and had come to seize the crown from the Yorkist king, Richard III (see page 12). Three weeks later Henry's army defeated and killed Richard at Bosworth in Leicestershire. This battle ended the Wars of the Roses between the families of Lancaster and York and marked the beginning of the reign of the first Tudor king, Henry VII.

To the Welsh, the battle was more than just a victory of one royal family over another. Henry was a Welshman as well as a Lancastrian. The Welsh had inhabited England before being driven out by Saxon (English) invaders in the fifth century. To have a Welsh king seemed to them a way of winning back England from the English. This is why thousands of Welsh troops joined Henry on his march into England. Soon after his victory, Henry married Elizabeth of York, hoping to unite the two royal families. He named their first son Arthur after a Welsh hero – the legendary 'King Arthur' – who was believed to have led a brave resistance against the Saxons around AD 500.

Henry was a wise king who kept the peace and ruled justly. During his reign trade prospered and rebellions were

QUESTIONS

1 The battle of Bosworth occurred at the end of the summer. In those days battles were often fought around that time of year. Can you think of any reasons why?

2 After his victory at Bosworth, what did Henry VII do to put a stop to the Wars of the Roses?

3 Do Henry VIII's pastimes (Source 2) tell you anything about his character?

4 What use might the ambassador's report (Source 2) have been to his government?

crushed. Both the King and his better-off subjects made money; Henry left a fortune when he died in 1509. He was succeeded, not by Arthur, who had died young, but by his second son, Henry. King Henry VIII, although born and brought up in England, was proud he was Welsh. He seemed like a fairy-tale prince after his sensible but rather dull father (**Source 2**).

Defender of the Faith

Henry VIII was a tall, powerful man, fond of showing off and keen to impress other kings by going to war. His chief minister, Cardinal Thomas Wolsey, helped to put such grand ideas in his head. In 1512 Henry joined the emperor of Germany in a war against France. The result was a disappointment for Henry. His troops captured a town and won a battle but the emperor let him down by making peace with the French behind his back. To make matters worse, the war proved more expensive than expected. Henry found he had spent the money left him by his father.

While Henry was away, an English army won a far greater victory – over the Scots at the battle of Flodden, near Berwick (1513). The King of Scotland, James IV, was killed, along with his son and thousands of his troops. This disastrous defeat meant Scotland had no adult monarch for many years to come.

In 1517 a bitter religious quarrel broke out in Germany where discontent with the Church was widespread. A monk named Martin Luther, angry at the rich and sinful lives led by the Pope and his cardinals, challenged the Church. Churchmen said that people would only be saved (go to heaven when they died) if they did what the Church told them. This meant attending services regularly, confessing their sins and, if possible, going on pilgrimages. Luther said this was not true; the way to heaven was to be found in the Bible. Anything not in the Bible was not to be believed. It was the one, sure guide for Christians because it had been inspired by God.

> **SOURCE 2**
> Here is part of a report about Henry VIII which the ambassador from Venice sent to his government in 1520.
>
> His Majesty is twenty-nine years old and extremely handsome … He is very accomplished, a good musician, composes well, is a most capital horseman, a fine jouster, speaks good French, Latin and Spanish, is very religious … He never hunts without tiring eight or ten horses a day, which he has stationed beforehand along the line of country he means to take … He is extremely fond of tennis, at which game it is the prettiest thing in the world to see him play.

Pope Leo X *excommunicated* Luther (expelled him from the Church). Luther was also condemned by the German emperor, Charles V, and had to go into hiding. He set about translating the Bible into German and also wrote books explaining his ideas. These books were soon selling in their thousands and Luther's message spread quickly across Europe. Christians who remained loyal to the Church were known as Catholics. Those who followed

> **SOURCE 3**
> In this painting, which dates from 1536, the four men throwing stones at the Pope are Matthew, Mark, Luke and John, the writers of the four Gospels.

Henry VIII, Reformation and Union with Wales 17

SOURCE 4

As a young man, Henry VIII loved riding in tournaments, where riders showed their skill in *jousting* (mock battles on horseback with blunted lances). The contestants tried to unhorse each other by charging down opposite sides of a wooden barrier. Here we see Henry riding 'for the love of the Queen' in a tournament in 1512. Catherine of Aragon had just given birth to a boy, but he died soon afterwards.

Luther and similar rebels were called Protestants because they protested against the Church. Soon wars and persecution raged over the Continent. Both sides behaved with great cruelty because they believed that only their faith would get a person to heaven.

Henry VIII sided with the Pope and wrote a book to prove Luther wrong. He gave a copy to the Pope who rewarded him with the title *Fidei Defensor*, which is Latin for 'Defender of the Faith'. A shortened form of this, FID DEF or FD, has been engraved on many British coins since.

The King's Great Matter

At first the pleasure-loving young King was content to let his Chancellor, Cardinal Wolsey, run the country. Many people thought the Cardinal was more powerful than the King but this was not so. Henry knew that Wolsey's pride had made him many enemies who would be pleased to see him fall.

Wolsey fell from power in the end through what was known as 'The King's Great Matter' – his wish to divorce his wife, Catherine of Aragon. The couple had been married for twenty years but only one of their children, Princess Mary, had survived. The King wanted a son; he was sure a woman could not keep order in England. He had also fallen in love with Anne Boleyn, a lively young lady-in-waiting to the Queen (**Source 5**). Obviously, Anne was more likely to give him a son than the ageing Catherine, so Henry asked the Pope, Clement VII, for a divorce.

The King's excuse for wanting to divorce Catherine was that she had been married to his brother Arthur first. To marry a brother's widow was against Church law. The Pope had allowed Henry's marriage only because Catherine swore she had never had intercourse with Arthur during their very short married life. Henry had always believed this. Now he said he was not so sure!

There was supposed to be no such thing as divorce in those days, but popes usually found a way round the problem if monarchs were involved. This time, however, it was not so easy. Clement had sided with

SOURCE 5

1528–9 Anne Boleyn stayed away from court because of gossip about her relationship with Henry. He wrote the following to her at this time.

I beseech you now, with the greatest earnestness, to let me know your whole intention as to the love between us two. I must … obtain this answer from you, having been for a whole year struck with the dart of love … No more to you at the present time, mine own darling, for lack of time, but that I wish you were in my arms … for I think it too long since I kissed you.

France in a war with the Emperor Charles V and the French had lost. For a time he was in the power of the Emperor, whose troops had captured Rome in 1527. Charles was Catherine's nephew. He dismissed talk of a divorce as an insult to his family.

Clement played for time, hoping that Henry would change his mind. A cardinal, Lorenzo Campeggio, was sent to England to judge Henry's case. He soon realised his task was hopeless. Henry, he remarked, would not believe his marriage was lawful if an angel told him so. Catherine was just as obstinate in claiming it *was* lawful (**Source 6**). Wolsey was blamed for this failure. The King expected him to have more influence with the Pope. Wolsey was dismissed as Henry's chief minister and, later, ordered to the Tower. He would have been executed had he not died in Leicester on his way to London in November 1530.

In 1532 Anne became pregnant. Marriage between the two lovers was essential if the child was to be a lawful heir to the throne. So Henry defied the Pope and broke Church law. In January 1533 he married Anne in a secret ceremony conducted by Thomas Cranmer, Archbishop of Canterbury. In May, Anne was crowned queen even though Catherine was still alive. On 7 September she gave birth to a girl, the future Queen Elizabeth I. The King was bitterly disappointed. Soon afterwards Clement excommunicated Henry.

The Reformation Parliament

Henry had called Parliament in 1529 as he wanted to get the support of his subjects in the quarrel with the Pope. He knew that many important families were against the Church's power and wealth and therefore likely to be on his side. In any case it was not difficult to arrange for men who agreed with the King to be chosen as MPs (**Source 8**).

The rebellion against the Church led by Luther is called the Reformation. It was a quarrel about religious belief. Henry's

SOURCE 6

Queen Catherine appeared before the King and Cardinal Campeggio at a special court held at Blackfriars in London. On 21 June 1529 she said this to Henry before walking out.

Sir, I beseech you for all the loves that hath been between us, and for the love of God, let me have justice and right … This twenty years I have been your true wife … and by you have several children, although it pleased God to call them out of this World, which was not my fault … When you had me first, I take God to be my judge, I was a true maid (virgin) … If there be any just cause by the law … against me, I am content to depart … If there be none, I beg let me remain your wife …

SOURCE 7

Cardinal Thomas Wolsey. He was the son of a butcher who rose to be Lord Chancellor and Archbishop of York through the King's favour. He became very rich and lived in grand style with hundreds of servants.

SOURCE 8

We can get some idea of how members of the House of Commons were chosen from this letter written by Christopher More to Thomas Cromwell, the King's chief minister, in March 1539.

My lord admiral has informed me that your pleasure is to have a friend of yours to be one of the [members] of the Parliament for the borough of Gatton in Surrey ... Your lordship shall have your way. I had promised it unto a friend of mine, which, since I know your lordship's pleasure, at my desire is contented to leave it ... If I might know the name of your lordship's friend, I shall ... make the arrangements.

SOURCE 9

Thomas Cromwell (1485–1540) was at various times a soldier, banker and lawyer. He served as Wolsey's secretary before becoming the King's chief minister. He was clever, cold and ruthless in dealing with his opponents.

quarrel with the Pope was not about religion but about who should rule the English Church. Nevertheless it is known as the English Reformation, and the Parliament which met from 1529 until 1536 is called the Reformation Parliament. This Parliament did all that Henry asked. To some, it seemed like a puppet whose strings were worked by the King's Chancellor, Thomas Cromwell – who had replaced Wolsey as chief minister. However this was not entirely true because many of its members strongly supported the changes Henry wanted to make.

The Reformation Parliament stopped the payment of taxes to the Pope and fined English clergymen for obeying him. In 1534 it made Henry 'Supreme Head of the Church in England'. Government officials who said the King had no right to this title were executed. At the same time, however, Henry remained a Catholic in his beliefs and persecuted Protestants when he caught them. The only change in worship he did allow was the use of an English translation of the Bible in churches (**Source 11**).

Dissolution of the Monasteries

Henry knew that defying the Pope was dangerous. The Catholic countries of Europe might use it as an excuse to attack England. He therefore needed money to strengthen his army and navy (**Source 12**).

QUESTIONS

1. Why was Henry VIII so disappointed by the birth of his daughter Elizabeth?
2. Does Source 8 tell you anything about Thomas Cromwell?
3. What message is Source 10 meant to give about Henry VIII and the changes he made to the English Church?
4. In what ways does Source 11 help to explain the spread of Protestant beliefs?

SOURCE 10

The 'Great Bible' of 1539 was issued with this engraving. It shows the King, with Cranmer and Cromwell on either side of him, giving Bibles to a grateful people who are shouting 'Vivat Rex' (the Latin for 'Long live the King'.)

To raise extra taxes would make him unpopular. Cromwell suggested a way round the problem. What if the monasteries – 502 abbeys, 136 nunneries and 187 friaries – were seized and closed down? Monastic land covered nearly a quarter of England and Wales. Monastic property included buildings, farms, livestock and a treasure house of gold and silver.

What excuse could Henry give for closing the monasteries? For many years people had complained that monks and nuns did not live as they should. They were sup-

SOURCE 11

Being able to read the Bible in English allowed people to make up their own minds about religious matters. However this often led to arguments in families. The following story was told by John Maldon himself.

When the King allowed the Bible to be read in all churches … John Maldon of Chelmsford in Essex, being but fifteen years old, came every Sunday to hear it. His father, seeing this, angrily fetched him away and told him to say his morning service in Latin instead … One night, his father being asleep, Maldon and his mother discussed the cross, whether one should kneel to it … Maldon told his mother this was Idolatry (worship of idols) and was against the will of God as written in the Bible. His mother told his father who beat him unmercifully.

SOURCE 12

Deal Castle, in Kent – one of 19 artillery forts built by Henry VIII between 1538 and 1542 against the risk of invasion.

posed to spend their days working, attending church services and praying to a strict timetable. But some failed in their duties. They missed services and gave time to worldly pleasures and vices. On the other hand, many monks and nuns lived holy lives and worked hard farming their lands, teaching the young, and caring for the poor, sick and homeless.

Cromwell was given the title Vicar-General of the Church. He sent out 'visitors' (inspectors) to each monastery.

SOURCES 13 AND 14

Cromwell got information about the monasteries not only from his 'visitors' (Source 13) but also from monks telling tales. One of these, Richard Beerly, was a monk at Pershore (Source 14).

13 We came to Glastonbury (in Somerset) on Friday ... And because his (the Abbot's) answers were not to our purpose we ... proceeded that night to search his study for letters and books and found ... a written book against the divorce of the King's Majesty ... which we take to be a great matter ... We have in money £300 ... a fair chalice (cup) of gold, and other pieces of plate, which the Abbot had hid.

14 Now I will instruct you somewhat of religious men ... Monks (at Pershore monastery in Worcestershire) drink ... after breakfast till ten or twelve of the clock, and come to matins (morning service) drunk as mice ... and some [play] at cards, and some at dice ... They do nothing for God ... I beseech you find me some other employment and save my soul.

These men were told to look for slack behaviour and sinful living. They did their job well (**Sources 13 and 14**). Greedy, lazy and dishonest monks, even monks and nuns who lived together as man and wife, were soon discovered. Cromwell put such bad reports before Parliament. The Lords and Commons pretended to be surprised and horrified. They passed laws to close the smaller monasteries; the great abbeys were destroyed later.

Between 1534 and 1539 about 10,000 monks and nuns were thrown out. Abbey lands were sold and the buildings put to other uses or knocked down. Abbots and monks who went quietly were given a pension and sometimes another job. Some of those who protested were executed. Henry's government sold the monastic lands to nobles and gentlemen, making about £1,500,000 – a fortune in those days.

The Pilgrimage of Grace

In the south of England the monastery closures went fairly smoothly. In the North it was a different story. Here people disliked 'interference' from the government in London and a King who had never even visited them. In 1536 a rebellion broke out in Yorkshire. The rebel army, calling itself the 'Pilgrimage of Grace', captured several towns including York. The leader of the 'pilgrims', a lawyer named Robert Aske, wanted the monasteries opened again and 'evil' advisers such as Cromwell punished (**Source 15**). It was autumn and heavy rain had made the roads in these hilly regions a sea of mud. A royal army led by the Duke of Norfolk was sent to crush the rebellion. It became bogged down.

Henry sensed danger. He ordered Norfolk to promise the rebels anything they wanted provided they agreed to go home. Aske trusted the King to keep his word so he persuaded the pilgrims to disperse. In January 1537 there was a small rising by a few discontented men. This gave Henry his chance. Although Aske and the other pilgrim leaders were not involved, the King held them responsible. Norfolk was ordered to march through the North doing 'dreadful execution'. Many pilgrims were killed in front of their wives and children. Aske was taken to York and hanged in chains. The most serious rebellion of Henry's reign had been crushed.

Henry's last years were spent fighting a costly war against the French. In 1544 his army invaded France and captured the town of Boulogne. Next year a large French fleet threatened the south coast of England. It was forced to withdraw after a sea-battle off the Isle of Wight. But Henry saw the pride of his fleet, the *Mary Rose*, sink suddenly outside Portsmouth harbour. Eighteen months later the King died (January 1547). His third wife, Jane Seymour, had given him a son, Edward. This nine year-old boy succeeded to the throne as Edward VI.

Welsh Acts of Union

Sir Rhys ap Thomas, who had fought alongside Henry VII at Bosworth, governed Wales for the Crown until 1525. His successor, Sir Rhys ap Gruffyd, ruled unfairly and gave the best jobs to his favourites. In 1531 he was executed. Wales was a wild and lawless country compared with England. In 1534 an English official in Wales begged Henry to send 'down to us some man to use the sword of justice, otherwise the Welsh will not be easy to bring to order'. He said the countryside was full of cattle-thieves and murderers, and people were forced to bar their doors and put scythes up their chimneys to keep intruders out.

Cromwell appointed Bishop Rowland Lee to take charge. Lee was a hard, strict

SOURCE 15

On 15 October 1536, Aske and his 'pilgrims' arrived outside York. When they found the gates shut against them, Aske issued this statement.

That certain evil persons, being of the King's council … intend to destroy the Church of England, and to spoil and rob the realm … We have taken this pilgrimage for the preservation of Christ's church, of this realm and the King, the nobility and commons … If you will not come on with us … we will fight and die against you and all those that shall try to stop us.

SOURCE 16

The sea battle against the French off the Isle of Wight, July 1545. The King is in the centre of the picture, while above we see the wreckage of *The Mary Rose*.

SOURCE 17

Henry VIII and his six wives: Catherine of Aragon – divorced; Anne Boleyn – executed for unfaithfulness; Jane Seymour – gave Henry his only son but died in childbirth; Anne of Cleves – divorced; Catherine Howard – executed for unfaithfulness; Catherine Parr – outlived the king.

1

2

3

5

4

6

man who disliked the Welsh. He is said to have hanged 5000 thieves and murderers and to have left the rest 'quaking with fear'. Such tough measures were followed by Acts of Parliament which joined Wales with England. The first Act of Union, in 1536, divided the whole of Wales into counties, like England. In future, English was to be the only language used in business and the law. And the Welsh custom of fathers dividing their land between their sons was replaced by the English custom of allowing the eldest son to inherit all the property.

In 1543 a further Act of Union set up a ruling council and lawcourts for Wales. Welsh courts could try all cases, including murder. Justices of the peace were appointed in the counties to deal with less serious offences. Finally, the Welsh were given a say in government for the first time. Each county and sizeable town was allowed to send two MPs to the House of Commons.

Wales was run more efficiently and fairly after the Union (**Source 19**). The harsh Rowland Lee was replaced as President of the Council for Wales by Sir Henry Sidney who grew to like the Welsh. During his rule the Bible was translated into Welsh (1588). The government hoped by this to encourage the Welsh people to become Protestants, but it also saved Welsh from dying out as a written language.

Union with England suited better-off Welsh families. They could get government jobs because they spoke English. They could trade with England and share in its growing prosperity. Many clever, well-educated Welsh people made a name for themselves in England. Poorer people, however, could not share these benefits. They were ruled by English laws and judged in courts where the officials used a language they could not understand. Their customs and way of life were changed to fit an English pattern. Wales was more peaceful and orderly after the Union. But the Welsh were not free from English rule, as some of the men who marched to Bosworth with Henry Tudor had hoped.

SOURCE 18

Sir Henry Sidney, President of the Council for Wales after the Union. He once claimed that it was his aim 'to do good every day.'

SOURCE 19

In 1594 a Welshman, George Owen, had this to say about the union with England fifty years before.

Now, since Wales was thus, by gracious King Henry VIII, united to England, and so brought to a monarchy, which is the most sure, stable and best form of government, they (the Welsh) are free from dangers ... for now life and death, land and goods rest in the safe hands of the monarchy ... Laws are written and therefore more certain to be truly administered ... The disputes between England and Wales then brought about slaughters, invasion, burnings, poverty and war. This union has produced friendship, love, alliance, assistance, wealth and quietness.

Henry VIII, Reformation and Union with Wales

Assessment tasks

A Knowledge and understanding

1. **a** How and why did Henry VIII's attitude towards the Pope change?
   b What effects did this have on religion in England?

2. Here are some reasons why Henry VIII closed the monasteries.

   - He had quarrelled with the Pope.
   - Many of his subjects were against monasteries.
   - He needed money.
   - To gain support among those who purchased monastic lands.
   - Monks' misbehaviour, reported by Cromwell's 'visitors'.
   - To reduce the power of the Church.

   Re-arrange these into what you consider to be their order of importance. Give reasons for your answer.

3. In what ways did the lives of ordinary people in Wales (a) get better, and (b) change for the worse, during Henry VIII's reign?

B Interpretations and sources

4. Source 19 gives one Welshman's view of the Union of England and Wales, fifty years or so after it happened. A further 400 years later, another Welshman wrote the following about the Union.

   > English was to be the only official language … No person or persons 'that use the Welsh speech shall have … or enjoy any manner of office (government job) within this realm' … In effect … people were made aliens (foreigners) in their own lawcourts … Welsh had to retreat to the kitchen … Many a [Welsh person] found himself cheerfully thumped about the head to the cry that Welshmen were now as free as Englishmen.
   > (Professor Gwyn A. Williams, 1985)

   Why do you think George Owen and Professor Williams see things so differently?

5. **a** What message is the painter of Source 3 trying to get across?
   b How does his message fit in with the teachings of Martin Luther?

6. Can you think of any reasons why Sources 13 and 14 may be unreliable?

3 Church and state

Elizabeth I, religion and Parliament

The statues pictured here (**Source 1**) were set up when England was a Catholic country. Protestants smashed them because they thought people should worship only Jesus Christ, not saints or the Virgin Mary. They were also afraid that some ignorant folk might be worshipping not just saints but the statues themselves. This was called *idolatry* and was forbidden in the Bible. Damage of this kind became widespread soon after Henry VIII died. His young son, Edward VI, became a keen Protestant. Unlike his father, who defied the Pope yet remained a Catholic, Edward wanted to wipe out all traces of Catholic worship.

Protestant reforms

To Catholics, a priest's job was to get Christians to heaven and save them from hell. Priests taught people how to lead good lives and made them take the *sacraments* (holy services). Sacraments were thought to be the way in which God's spirit entered a person. One of the most important sacraments was holy communion, given during the service of mass, when it was believed that the priest received the body and blood of Christ through the bread and wine.

Protestants did not believe sacraments were so important. For them, the way to heaven was through faith in Christ and this would come from studying God's word in the Bible. Protestants were against Catholic customs as well as beliefs. They wanted services to be plain and simple. They did not like statues, ornaments or paintings in a church. They did not light candles, burn incense or play organ music during prayers. Protestants objected to having bishops dressed in grand robes or priests in rich *vestments* (special clothing worn during services).

In 1549 Thomas Cranmer, Archbishop of Canterbury, issued a new Prayer Book written in English, not Latin. This set out the way services and prayers were to be carried out in churches. All ornaments and statues were to be taken out of churches and paintings covered with whitewash. Protestants were delighted. For the first time they were able to worship openly.

SOURCE 1

These statues of the Virgin Mary and St Michael in the parish church of Coslany, near Norwich, were broken during the Reformation.

SOURCE 2

The boy king, Edward VI, in 1548. His father, Henry VIII, who died in the previous year, is shown on the left. To the right of Edward we see his uncle, the Duke of Somerset, who was 'Lord Protector', and other members of the ruling council. The picture was painted to celebrate an order to destroy religious statues.

People who preferred the old ways were puzzled and horrified. They thought the sights and sounds in a church – the paintings, statues and singing – put them in touch with God. They liked the sound of the Latin prayers even if they did not understand them. Many priests thought the same and there were serious rebellions against the new Prayer Book in Oxfordshire and the West Country (**Source 3**). These were crushed, however, and England seemed well on the way to becoming a Protestant country when Edward died, aged 16, in 1553.

Mary – the Catholic Queen

Edward's death led to a complete change. Mary, who succeeded her brother, was the only surviving child of Henry VIII's first marriage, to Catherine of Aragon. She shared her mother's strict Catholic views. Mary banned the new Prayer Book and ordered everyone to worship as Catholics. Many Protestant clergymen fled abroad. Archbishop Cranmer and other Protestant bishops were put in prison. Protestants who stuck to their faith openly were burned as *heretics* (non-believers). At least 270 men and women, including Cranmer, died in this way (**Source 4**).

Mary was determined that England should never be Protestant again. She declared the Pope head of the English Church once more and looked for a husband, so that she could have children to carry on her work. From Mary's point of view there could be no better choice than the Catholic Prince Philip, future king of Spain. In 1554 she married Philip in Winchester Cathedral.

The 'Spanish marrige' was very unpopu-

28   Church and state

lar in England. As wives were supposed to obey their husbands, English people complained that they now had a foreign ruler. Rebels tried to stop the wedding but they were defeated and their leaders executed. The marriage itself was a failure. Philip soon returned to Spain and the child Mary longed for never came. Lonely and unhappy, she died in November 1558 and her younger sister, Elizabeth, became queen.

SOURCE 4

In 1562 John Foxe, a Protestant clergyman, published a book about the sufferings of Christian *martyrs* (people who die for their faith). Here Foxe describes the death, in 1555, of two Protestant bishops, Hugh Latimer and Nicholas Ridley.

Then they brought a faggot (firewood), set it alight and laid it down at Ridley's feet. To Ridley, Latimer spoke in this way ... 'Be of good comfort, brother Ridley, and play the man; we shall this day light such a candle in England as I trust shall never be put out' ... Latimer soon died, as it appears with little pain ... But Ridley lingered for the fire burned all his lower parts before it touched the upper.

SOURCE 3

Rebels against the new Prayer Book sent these demands to London, in July 1549, while they were besieging the town of Exeter.

The demands of the commons (ordinary people) of Devon and Cornwall, sent to the King ... We will have the mass in Latin, as was before... We will have holy bread and holy water made every Sunday, and palms (for Palm Sunday) and ashes (for Ash Wednesday) as usual. We will have images set up in churches, and the old ceremonies ... We will not receive the new service because it is but like a Christmas game ... We will have the Bible and all books in English to be called in.

SOURCE 5

Queen Mary with Prince Philip of Spain. Mary was eleven years older than her husband.

QUESTIONS

1. In Source 3, what do you think the rebels meant when they described the new service as 'like a Christmas game'?
2. What parts of Source 4 suggest that it was probably based on an account by an eyewitness?
3. Why did Mary consider Philip of Spain to be such a suitable husband?
4. Many people in England were thankful that Mary died childless. Can you explain why?

SOURCE 6

John Calvin. His rule in Geneva was very strict. Inspectors visited homes to find out if anything immoral was going on. A girl who put non-religious words to a hymn tune was whipped; a boy who struck his parents was beheaded. English Protestants who took refuge in Geneva during Mary's reign came under Calvin's influence.

The Elizabethan Church

Elizabeth was Anne Boleyn's daughter, born while Catherine of Aragon was still alive (see Chapter 2). To the Pope and many foreign Catholics, she had no right to be queen. The Catholic King of France, Henry II, announced that Mary Stuart, Queen of Scotland, was the rightful ruler of England. Mary was Elizabeth's cousin and her nearest relative. But the English people would not be told by foreigners who should rule them. They rallied round the new Queen. Supported by Parliament, Elizabeth was made Supreme Governor of the Church of England in 1559.

Elizabeth, knowing her people were divided about religion, tried to satisfy both sides. A new English Prayer Book was issued, similar to those used in Edward's reign. The Catholic mass was replaced by a Protestant communion service. In this worshippers took the bread and wine, not as the body and blood of Christ, but simply to remember that Christ died for them on the cross. At the same time many Catholic customs remained, including rule by bishops, sacraments, vestments for priests, church ornaments and music.

Everyone had to attend such services. Catholics who refused were called *recusants* (which means they disobeyed authority) and fined 12 pence for every absence from church. Rules of this kind about religion were usual in those days. Every government expected its people to worship in the same way and believe the same things about God. In England, after 1559, it was not possible to be a lawyer, schoolteacher, university student, Member of Parliament or government official unless you went to church regularly and took an oath saying that the Queen was head of the Church.

Obviously Catholics were against the Elizabethan Church, but so were many Protestants. For some it was still too Catholic in its ways. They wanted to 'purify' the Church of such customs and so were known as *puritans*. A few wanted to do away with bishops altogether and have a church run by elected committees of *presbyters* (elders, or teachers). Presbyterian churches of this kind had been set up by a Protestant leader, John Calvin, in Switzerland.

Elizabeth actually liked Catholic-style worship and disliked puritans. She was determined not to give in to them. But puritan ideas, often supported by wealthy and educated men, spread during her reign. Secret meetings, called prophesyings, were held. At these the congregation read and discussed texts from the Bible. The authorities broke up such meetings when they could and prosecuted those responsible (**Source 7**).

The Society of Jesus

In 1570 the Pope excommunicated Elizabeth and called for her overthrow. From then on life became increasingly difficult for English Catholics. Although most were loyal to the Queen, it was easy for their enemies to brand them as traitors working to destroy the government. Reluctantly, Elizabeth was forced to tighten the laws against Catholics. Fines for recusants were increased until they reached £260 a year. Catholic priests were declared traitors and banned from the country.

A few brave men ignored the ban and slipped into England in disguise. Some were Jesuits – members of The Society of Jesus – who were trained to die for their faith if necessary. Jesuits claimed that they only came to England to hold services for Catholic families in their homes. The government said they were missionaries who came to convert Protestants.

One of the first Jesuits to arrive in England, in 1580, was Edmund Campion. In his youth, while he was a student at Oxford University, his cleverness had been admired by the Queen. For a time he dodged the authorities, but in 1581 he was captured (**Source 8**). Campion had done nothing except preach the Catholic faith. But because he supported the Pope – an enemy of the Queen – he was found guilty of treason and hanged.

Elizabeth and her parliaments

Elizabeth held ten parliaments during her reign (1558–1603). She called them for various reasons, often because she was short of money. Parliament passed the Acts to establish the Church of England. Its members also tried to arrange the succession to the throne and raised taxes for a war with Spain. Several times groups of lords and MPs asked the Queen to consider marriage. If she died childless, Mary Stuart would be next in line to the throne and this might lead to civil war between Protestants and Catholics.

SOURCE 7

In June 1567 a prophesying meeting of about 100 people was raided by the authorities and the ringleaders arrested. Next day they were taken before Edmund Grindal, Bishop of London. Here is part of the hearing.

BISHOP GRINDAL You have showed yourself disorderly, not only in being absent from your parish churches ... but also you have gathered together, made assemblies, even ministered the sacraments yourselves ...

JOHN SMITH *(one of the accused)* We never assembled together for preaching until all our preachers were sacked by your law so we could hear none of them in any church. We heard of a congregation in Geneva (Switzerland) which used a Bible and order of preaching most agreeable to the word of God ... which book and order we now obey. If you can prove this Bible, or anything we believe, wrong, we will give way to you ... If not, we stand to it by the grace of God.

SOURCE 8

This letter was written by the Jesuit priest, Edmund Campion, soon after his arrival in England. The *heretics* (non-believers) he refers to were the Protestant authorities.

I cannot long escape the hands of the heretics; the enemy has so many eyes ... I wear ridiculous clothes ... I often change my name ... I read letters (news sheets) that tell news that Campion is captured, which I hear in every place ... I have published the reasons why I have come. I have asked for a debate with the Queen but am told the Queen will not allow [religious] matters, already decided, to be questioned ... Very many are being restored to the Church.

Elizabeth probably never intended to marry, but she kept everyone guessing, courting several foreign princes and flirting with her favourite, Robert Dudley, Earl of Leicester (**Source 10**). As she grew older, the Commons gave up hope of her having children but begged her to name a successor. She never did and never got married. Elizabeth remains England's only 'Virgin Queen'.

The Queen tried to run the House of Commons through her ministers, but such control was not easy. By custom, the Commons asked the monarch for freedom of speech before each session. Publicly, Elizabeth always said yes. Privately, however, she made it clear that she wished to limit discussion of certain topics, including foreign affairs and religion. These were

SOURCE 9

Parliament in the reign of Elizabeth I. Can you identify the Lords and Commons?

SOURCE 10

In 1566 Parliament presented a *petition* (request) to Elizabeth about her marriage and the succession to the throne. She gave this angry reply.

I say again, I will marry as soon as I can conveniently, if God take not him away with whom I wish to marry, or God take myself, or something else happen ... And I hope to have children, otherwise I would never marry ... Your petition [also] deals with the succession to the throne. If you did have freedom to decide this, there would be so many competitors [for the Crown] that there should be some peril to you, and certain danger to me.

SOURCE 11

This is part of Peter Wentworth's speech, made in the House of Commons on 8 February 1576.

Mr Speaker, two things do great harm to this place. The one is the rumour which runneth about the House, and that is, 'Take heed what you do, the Queen liketh not such a matter ...' The other was a message that we should not debate any matters of religion, but first to receive [instructions] from the Bishop. Surely this was a miserable message; for it was as much as to say, 'Sir, you shall not debate God's causes, no, nor seek to improve His Glory'.

QUESTIONS

1. Why were Catholic priests declared traitors?
2. In Source 8, what sentence appears to contradict Campion's claim that he was only in England to serve Catholic families?
3. Why was the succession to the throne so important in those days? Why is it less important today?
4. Why do you think Elizabeth did not want religious matters to be debated in Parliament?

obviously important and some members refused to stay quiet about them. In 1576 a puritan MP, Peter Wentworth, made a speech saying the Queen interfered too much (**Source 11**). The Commons felt Wentworth had gone too far and sent him to the Tower. The Queen was also furious but she soon released him.

Quarrels between the Queen and Parliament never got out of hand because both Commons and Lords adored her. She was admired even by puritans. In November 1601, in her last speech to Parliament, she said: 'And though God has raised me so high, yet this I count the glory of my Crown, that I have reigned with your loves'. Those who heard her that day agreed that this was true.

Quarrel with Spain

Philip, who had been married to Mary, became King of Spain in 1555. Catholic Spain was an immensely rich and powerful country in those days, ruling the largest empire in the world. Its territories included the Netherlands, much of America and parts of Italy. Philip was very religious; he believed that God had given him great power for the purpose of defeating Protestants everywhere.

At first, Philip hoped to get the changes he desired in England by marrying Elizabeth. When she turned him down he encouraged plots against her. Most of these centred round putting the Catholic Queen of Scotland, Mary Stuart, on the throne. In 1568 Mary, after an unhappy reign, was driven out of Scotland because people suspected her of murdering her husband, Lord Darnley. She fled to England where Elizabeth treated her with respect but locked her up.

Mary's arrival in England encouraged further plots against the English Queen. Elizabeth's advisers urged her, for her own safety, to put Mary to death, but she resisted the idea of killing a close relative and a queen. Elizabeth's patience finally ran out in 1586 when a group of Catholics led by Anthony Babington planned to kill her and

SOURCE 12

Mary Stuart, Queen of Scots. The Scottish people turned against her when she was believed to have plotted the death of her husband, Lord Darnley, in order to marry his suspected murderer, the Earl of Bothwell.

SOURCE 13

Here is part of a letter Mary Stuart wrote in reply to Babington. It was in code but government agents deciphered it.

I cannot but praise your desire to hinder the plans of our enemies who seek to destroy our religion in this realm ... Long ago I pointed out to other foreign Catholic princes that the longer we delayed intervening [in England], the greater the advantage to our opponents. Meanwhile the Catholics here, exposed to all kinds of cruelty, steadily grow less in numbers and power ... Everything being prepared, and the forces being ready ... I must in some way be got from here ... to await foreign assistance.

release Mary. They contacted Mary with coded letters hidden in beer barrels. These were found, along with Mary's replies, and decoded by government spies.

Babington and the other plotters were hanged, drawn and quartered. On the evidence of her letters (**Source 13**), Mary was put on trial, found guilty and condemned to death. For some time Elizabeth could not bring herself to sign the death warrant. But at last Mary was beheaded at Fotheringay Castle in Northamptonshire on 8 February 1587.

For Philip, the death of Mary was the last straw. Over the years he had been annoyed by raids by English seamen on Spanish colonies and ships. And when his Protestant subjects in Holland rebelled, Elizabeth interfered on the rebels' side and finally sent an army to assist the Dutch in their struggle. In 1588 Philip hit back. He sent an Armada (fleet) of 130 ships, carrying 8000 soldiers, to conquer England. The Spanish plan was to sail from Lisbon to the English Channel, seize Margate in Kent and ferry a Spanish army across from Holland.

In July 1588, the Armada moved slowly up the Channel. But when it anchored off Calais to wait for the Spanish army, the English attacked with 'fireships'. These were empty ships, filled with tar and gunpowder, which were set alight and sent downwind towards the enemy. To escape destruction, the Spanish captains cut their anchors and headed out to sea in all directions.

A fierce battle between the English and Spanish fleets raged for six days off Gravelines, near Dunkirk. The Armada, badly battered, was driven into the North Sea and forced to sail home round the coasts of Scotland and Ireland. The sick and wounded, with nothing but rotting food to eat and foul water to drink, suffered terribly. Fifty-three ships and a third of the men never reached home. It was a crushing defeat and Protestants were sure it showed God was on their side (**Source 17**).

SOURCE 14

Mary Stuart's execution, drawn by an eyewitness. Outside, servants are shown burning her clothes.

34 Church and state

SOURCE 15

In this painting from St Faith's Church in King's Lynn, Norfolk, we see Queen Elizabeth speaking to her troops at Tilbury (see page 36) and, behind, scenes from the battle against the Armada. The Spanish galleons have been set on fire by the English fireships.

Route of the Spanish Armada

Elizabeth I, religion and Parliament

SOURCE 16

This portrait of Queen Elizabeth was painted to celebrate victory over the Spanish Armada. She is shown wearing pearls that her favourite, the Earl of Leicester, gave her.

SOURCE 17

In August 1588, Elizabeth made this speech to her army assembled at Tilbury, near London, ready for a Spanish invasion.

I am come amongst you at this time, not for my recreation or sport, but being resolved (determined) in the midst and heat of battle to live and die amongst you all ... I know I have the body of a weak and feeble woman, but I have the heart and courage of a king, and of a king of England too, and think foul scorn that Parma (the Spanish general in Holland) or Spain, or any prince of Europe, should dare to invade ... my realm.

Assessment tasks

A Knowledge and understanding

1 Mary and Elizabeth were the first two reigning queens of England. In what ways do you think they were (a) at an advantage, and (b) at a disadvantage, as a result of being women?

2 a Using information in the last two chapters, make a timeline to show the main steps by which England became a Protestant country.
  b From the point of view of ordinary churchgoers, what sorts of things remained the same in spite of the English Reformation?

3 What was the most important reason why King Philip of Spain sent his Armada against England in 1588? You may wish to choose one of the following. Give reasons for your answer.

- English raids on Spanish colonies and shipping.
- He wanted to rule England.
- The execution of Mary Stuart.
- To make England Catholic again.
- English support for the Dutch revolt.
- He was annoyed that Elizabeth would not marry him.

B Interpretations and sources

4 Here two modern historians give their opinion of Mary Stuart's part in the Babington conspiracy of 1586 (see Source 13).

> On 17 July the answer (to Babington) was written. It was an exceedingly long letter, warmly welcoming the plot and the slaying of Elizabeth ... Damning enough if read by itself, it was fatal when read with Babington's letter ... There can be no doubt whatever that Mary had consented to a plot to assassinate the Queen and to bring an invading army into England. She ... denied it; ... that was natural, for she was fighting for her life.
> (J.E. Neale, 1960)

> It is certainly possible ... to forgive Mary ... her own agreement [to] a conspiracy involving the assassination of Elizabeth ... may be compared to the actions of a prisoner who is prepared to escape by a certain route even if it may involve the slaying of the jailor ... If her own life in captivity could be considered in danger, then there was much doubt as to whether agreeing to slay Elizabeth was sinful at all.
> (Antonia Fraser, 1969)

What are the differences between these accounts? How might such differences be explained?

5 Look carefully at Source 2 and then answer the following questions.

  a Why do you think Henry VIII is shown in the picture?
  b Why is Henry pointing at Edward?
  c Who is the man being struck by a book at the bottom of the picture, and what is the book meant to be?
  d What is happening in the upper right hand corner?
  e Why are the two figures at the bottom (left) looking unhappy?
  f What message do you think this painting is meant to give?

6 Re-read Source 10 and then answer the following questions.
  a What does this source tell you about Elizabeth's attitude to marriage?
  b If Parliament had been allowed to settle the succession to the throne, how could this have put Elizabeth in danger?
  c What other source in this chapter suggests that Elizabeth might have been right about such danger?

Elizabeth I, religion and Parliament   37

4 Gloriana's people

Elizabethan life

> **SOURCE 1**
>
> Queen Elizabeth being carried to a wedding by nobles and gentlemen. This painting dates from 1600 – three years before her death.

Elizabeth was often lonely, worried and tired, but she rarely showed it. The outside world saw a proud woman, dressed in fine clothes and jewellery, sailing on the Thames in her barge or travelling through the countryside on summer *progresses* (royal tours). Artists painted her like a goddess. Poets called her 'Gloriana' (glorious). Courtiers spent vast sums of money entertaining her in their houses. She gave her name to a period of history – the Elizabethan Age.

Mansions, manor houses and cottages

With the coming of more peaceful times, most noble families now lived in mansions, not castles. The largest were like palaces, with tall towers, corkscrew chimneys, fancy weather vanes and carvings. Many were built in an E-shape in honour of Elizabeth. The great hall in such houses was rarely used for feasts, as it had been in earlier times. Families often ate in smaller rooms, some with names we still use today. The main bedchamber had a 'withdrawing room' next door. Here the servants slept within call of their master and mistress. From this we get our modern 'drawing room'. Another example is parlour, a room for chatting, which gets its name from the French word *parler*, to speak.

The most important room in the house was the gallery. This was a long, wide passage with windows on one side (**Source 2**). It was set in an upper storey and warmed by fireplaces. Portraits of members of the family were hung on one side and window seats set on the other to give a view of the gardens. Galleries were recreation places for both grown-ups and children. Here members of the family and their guests could walk, dance, fence or play games. The polished wooden floor we often see today in such houses would have been

SOURCE 2

Hardwick Hall in Derbyshire, built in the 1590s by a rich widow, Elizabeth, Countess of Shrewsbury. The ES on the towers stands for Elizabeth Shrewsbury. The long gallery is shown on the left.

SOURCE 3

A Tudor manor house: St Fagan's, near Cardiff. It has several large fireplaces and its glass windows would have been a luxury at the time.

strewn with sweet-smelling herbs in Elizabethan times.

Country gentlemen who had done well showed off their wealth by building manor houses, made of brick or stone. Town dwellings were usually set in terraces with a narrow front on the street and a long garden, or court, at the back. Yeomen who could not afford a manor house might build a new farmhouse or improve their old one. Even a humble labourer might add a partition to his cottage, to separate people and animals, or lay stone slabs over the mud floor. There were many such signs of increased wealth as the century wore on (**Source 4**).

'Keep some great man as a friend'

Lord Burghley, Elizabeth's chief minister, once told his son how to get on in life. 'Be sure to keep some great man as a friend', he said. It was good advice. The best 'friend' of all, of course, was the Queen.

SOURCE 4

William Harrison (1534–93) was a clergyman and a scholar. In 1577 he wrote a *Description of England*, from which this extract comes.

The ancient manors and houses of our gentlemen are of strong timber … Such as be built lately are either of brick or stone, or both; their rooms large and comfortable. Those of the nobility are … so magnificent and stately that a dog today has the same comforts as a prince of olden times … There are old men in the village where I live which have noted three things to be marvellously altered in England … One is the multitude of chimneys, whereas in their younger days there were not more than two or three … The second is the great improvement in lodging (homes). The third thing they tell is of the change from wooden platters (plates) into pewter, and wooden spoons into silver and tin.

QUESTIONS

1. At night, why do you think nobles liked to have servants within calling distance of their bedchamber?
2. Why would long galleries have been good places for hanging paintings?
3. In Source 4, what evidence does the writer give of increasing wealth in sixteenth-century England?
4. Do you think Shakespeare really believed that his poem was poor (Source 5)? If not, why did he write to the Earl of Southampton in this way?

She could make a man a lord, knight, bishop or judge. She could give her favourites land, a pension or a monopoly (the sole right to trade in a particular product). She also had about 200 jobs to fill in the royal household. In the same way, lords and knights had wealth and positions to give to their friends and relatives. All such favours and rewards were known as *patronage* because the monarch, lord or knight was said to be the patron of those they helped (**Source 5**).

Burghley used to receive 60 to 100 letters a day asking for some favour or other. He often rewarded those he thought would be able to help him in return. The Queen did the same. Her awards went to those who were loyal or whose help she needed. For example, many lords and MPs who voted for the 1559 Church Settlement (see Chapter 3) did so because they had been promised rewards from the Queen. On the other hand, to lose favour with the Queen often meant ruin or worse.

Many quite important government jobs were unpaid or had a small salary. The real 'wages' came when the official received gifts, which we would call bribes. These could take many forms, from land, gold or jewels to food, pets or just a bowl of fruit! Leicester and Burghley often complained that Elizabeth did not pay them much. Even so, Burghley could afford to build two of the grandest mansions in England – Grantham and Theobalds. And Leicester, the Queen's favourite, earned enough to spend a fortune before he died.

Poor Laws

During Tudor times the cost of living rose while the value of money dropped. If people made their living from rents on land or from trade this did not matter too much. If they were paid wages, however, they grew poorer as their few pence a week bought less. With more and more people close to starvation, Elizabethan governments were afraid that some might rebel. They started to pass laws to deal with the poor.

In earlier times monks had helped the poor. Now the monasteries were closed and monastic buildings left to fall into ruin. A way had to be found to provide jobs for the fit and care and shelter for the young, sick and old. By the middle of the century several town councils, including those in Norwich, Ipswich and London, decided that their better-off citizens must pay a 'poor rate' to help those who were penniless and without work (**Source 6**).

In 1563 Parliament passed a Statute of Artificers (craftsmen). This ordered most men and women between the ages of 12 and 60 to work on the land. It even laid down the hours of work, from 5.00 am to 7.30 pm in the summer and dawn to dusk in the winter. Boys had to serve a seven-year apprenticeship to a trade. Those who passed this Act thought that if people were organised properly there would be enough work to go round. Therefore, those without work were just 'idle rogues' who must be punished. In 1572 it was ordered that such 'vagrants' were to be rounded up. They were to be flogged or have their ears

> **SOURCE 5**
> In 1593 young William Shakespeare, hoping to make a career as a writer, published a poem called *Venus and Adonis*. It was dedicated to his *patron* as follows.
>
> To the Right Honourable Henry Wriothesley, Earl of Southampton and Baron of Titchfield … I know not how I shall offend in dedicating my poem to your lordship, nor how the world will censure (criticise) me for choosing so strong a prop [as you] to support so weak a burden [as my poem]; only if your honour seem but pleased, I account myself highly praised, and promise to take advantage of all idle hours, till I have honoured you with some graver labour (better poem) … Your honour's in all duty, William Shakespeare.

> **SOURCE 6**
> Here the town council of Norwich explains why it started to collect a compulsory poor rate.
>
> The city of Norwich had [on] many occasions demanded that there be better provision for the poor … The citizens felt themselves aggrieved (complained) that the city was so full of poor people who … used church porches, men's cellars, doors, barns and hay chambers to bestow themselves (sleep) … and what with disease … their flesh was eaten with vermin and corruption … A great sort came to waste (many died).

SOURCE 7

In this book illustration dating from 1577 we see a 'vagabond' being flogged through the streets for begging. Notice that he is shown as a fit, strong man, presumably able to work. On the left, another vagabond is being hanged – the final penalty for persistent begging.

bored through for begging. If they still did not go to work they were to be hanged.

'Vagrants' included not only those without work but also such people as pedlars (travelling salesmen), actors, minstrels and fortune-tellers. Wounded soldiers and sailors, however, were given a licence to beg. Also, parish authorities were allowed, if they wished, to build homes and hospitals for the sick and old, and they were ordered to find jobs for the workless. Throughout most of the 1570s and 80s, good harvests kept food cheap and so helped the poor. In the 1590s it was a different story. Bad harvests forced up the price of corn and led to widespread distress. For some, this was made worse by vagrants stealing food (**Source 8**).

The government decided to join all the different rules and regulations together into one great Poor Law, 1601. Under this Act every parish had to look after its own poor and larger parishes were to help smaller ones. Parish officials called *overseers* were appointed to collect the poor rate. Work was to be found for fit men and women, and poor children were to learn a craft or trade. Where necessary, 'workhouses' were to be provided to house the old and sick. This system lasted until the nineteenth century.

Schools and universities

In medieval times most boys from well-to-do families were educated in a lord's household or at a monastery. After the closing of the monasteries in the reign of Henry VIII, some monastic schools carried on as cathedral schools. During Elizabeth's reign many new schools were founded by wealthy men and women. By

SOURCE 8

Edward Hext, a Justice of the Peace in Somerset, reported as follows to Lord Burghley on 25 September 1596.

And this year there assembled 80 rogues ... and took a whole load of cheese from one countryman and ... shared it out amongst themselves ... They say that the rich men have got it all in their own hands and will starve the poor ... I say that the large numbers of idle, wandering people and robbers of the land are the chief cause of the food shortage, for they do not work but lie idly in ale-houses day and night eating and drinking excessively ... And when they are put in jail, the poor country people they have robbed are forced to feed them.

SOURCE 9

This woodcut from 1569 shows a wealthy gentleman rejecting the advances of a beggar.

SOURCE 10

Jesus College, University of Oxford – founded during the reign of Elizabeth, in 1571.

1600 there were 360 'grammar schools' in England and Wales. Most were small by today's standards, often with only 40 or 50 pupils.

Tudor education was meant to produce the 'perfect' lady or gentleman. Boys and girls were expected to be well-behaved and religious (**Source 11**). Teaching, both at home and in the school, was very strict. Lessons had to be learned by heart. If pupils did poor work, or could not remember something, they were flogged (**Source**

SOURCE 11

This advice was given to parents and teachers by Hugh Rhodes, in his *Book of Nurture, or School of Good Manners* (1577).

There are few things more necessary than to teach and govern children in learning and good manners, for it is a high service to God … [Parents should] cause their children and servants to use fair and gentle speech, with reverence and courtesy to their Elders and Betters [and tell them off] for idle talk and stammering, also clumsy gestures in going or standing … Keep them from reading fables, fantasies and songs of love which cause much mischief.

Elizabethan life

SOURCE 12

Richard Mulcaster was a famous Elizabethan headmaster. Here one of his former pupils, Thomas Fuller, describes his teaching methods.

His method of teaching was this. In the morning he would … [explain] the lesson to his scholars; which done, he slept an hour in his desk in the school, but woe to any scholar that slept … Awaking, he heard (tested) them accurately; and showed no pity where he found fault … It may truly be said … that others have taught as much learning with fewer lashes. Yet … many excellent scholars were bred under him.

SOURCE 13

The badge of Louth Grammar School, in Lincolnshire, dating from the Elizabethan period. It shows the importance of flogging in schools at that time!

SOURCE 14

Queen Elizabeth made the Earl of Leicester watch over Oxford University as its Chancellor. He took over in 1564 and at once set about restoring order among the students, as this letter to the college authorities shows.

The disorders concern no less than your religion … and the whole state of your university … These things are noted … lack of instructing your youth in the Principles of Religion … the allowing of secret Papists (Catholics) amongst you … Excess in apparel (over-dressing), as like silk and velvet … the Ale-houses full all day and much of the night with scholars drinking, dicing, carding and I will not say worse … Is this the ancient discipline of the university … to learn nothing else but to drink in taverns and leave knowing less than when they came?

12). Latin grammar was the main subject. This is how grammar schools got their name. A knowledge of Latin was vital. Every subject at university was taught in Latin and it was even used in business.

Boys usually went from grammar school to university at the age of fifteen or sixteen. Neither grammar schooling nor study at university were thought suitable for girls. They were expected to learn how to manage a household. Daughters of wealthy families had lessons from their mothers or from private tutors at home. The Queen's tutor, Roger Ascham, was a famous scholar who said she was his cleverest pupil.

There were only two universities in England, Oxford and Cambridge. However, lawyers often studied at the Inns of Court in London. Until the sixteenth century, only *graduates* (men who had passed their degree examinations) lived in the colleges at Oxford and Cambridge. Ordinary students lodged in hostels. But many of them were little more than schoolboys and were often difficult to control. There were frequent riots and fights with the townspeople. During Tudor times many colleges built study-bedrooms inside their grounds, set round a courtyard or quadrangle. The college gates could then be shut at night, locking the students in. Any caught out after this was flogged.

A student spent four years getting his bachelor's degree (BA) and another three for his Master of Arts (MA). The main subjects were religion, law, philosophy, medicine, dialectic (debating), geometry, astronomy, Greek and Hebrew. There were no written examinations. Candidates were asked questions and had to answer in Latin. Rich students rarely bothered to take the examinations. Poor students had no choice. They needed to be qualified for a job when they left. Tudor governments looked upon universities as places for training clergymen, lawyers and government officials, so they kept a close eye on them (Source 14).

44 Gloriana's people

The theatre

For many years plays were performed in the streets, at fairgrounds or in large houses and taverns. In 1576 James Burbage, a wealthy actor, built the first permanent theatre in England at Shoreditch in London. It was a success, so other theatres – the Globe, Swan and Curtain – were built on the south bank of the Thames, outside London's walls. Crowds spread diseases and theatre audiences were often very rough, so they were not allowed inside the City (**Source 15**).

It was not thought decent for women to act on the stage, so female parts were played by boys. Popular plays, including those by William Shakespeare, were written in English. However the Latin word 'Exit' over theatre doorways reminds us that plays in that language were performed in centres of learning – at Oxford, Cambridge and the Inns of Court.

William Shakespeare (1564–1616) was the most famous playwright of the time. He was born in Stratford-on-Avon in Warwickshire and went to London to be an actor. He wrote comedies, historical dramas and tragedies (plays with an unhappy ending). Elizabeth liked Shakespeare's plays. She was at the first performance of his *Twelfth Night* in 1601. Her favourite Shakespeare character was the fat, cowardly Sir John Falstaff, in

SOURCE 15

Thomas Nashe, in his *Pierce Penilesse* (1592), writes in support of playhouses.

Plays are very necessary ... [In] the afternoon, being the idlest time of day, men ... divide into gaming, drinking, or seeing a play: is it not better they should see a play? ... Most plays show the ill-success of treason, the fall of hasty climbers, the wretched end of usurpers (those who seize power illegally), the misery of civil war and how God is evermore punishing murder.

SOURCE 16

Drawing of the Swan Theatre, London, made in 1596. It was in theatres like this that Shakespeare's plays were performed.

QUESTIONS

1. What particular 'Principles of Religion' had the Earl of Leicester in mind (Source 14)? What do you think annoyed him most about the way Oxford University was being run?
2. Why would the Queen have agreed with the views expressed in Source 15?
3. Can you think of any reason why the Swan theatre (Source 16) was open to the sky?
4. What kinds of stories would Irish 'bards' and 'rhymers' be likely to tell (Source 18)? Why might the English have disliked such tales?

Elizabethan life

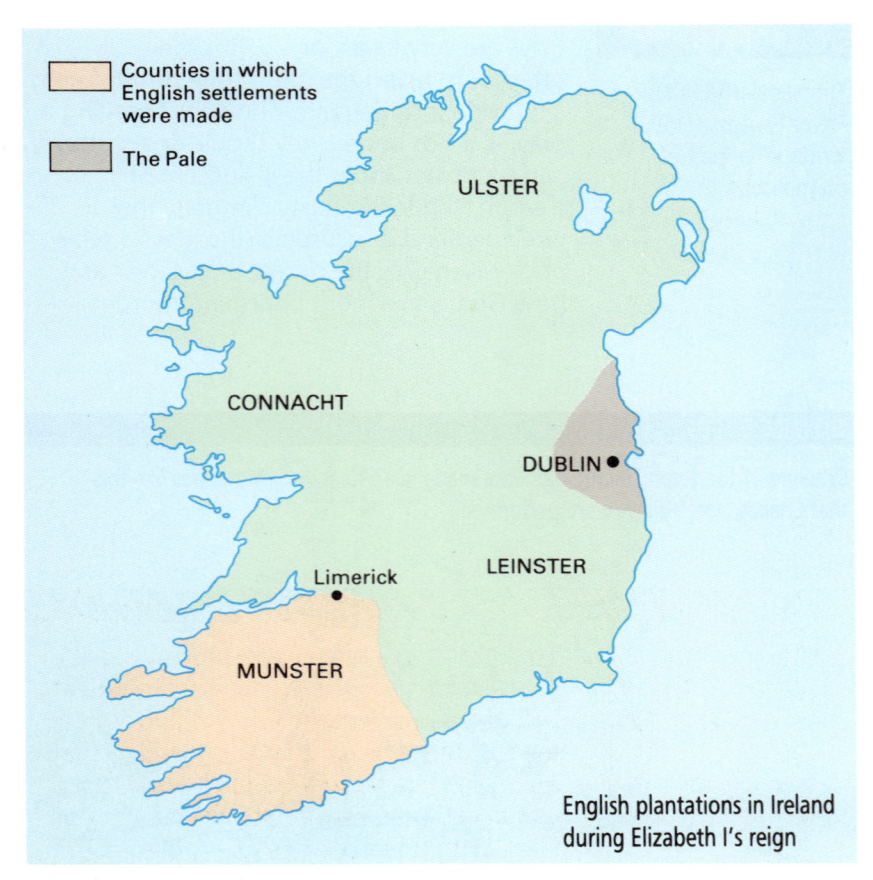

Counties in which English settlements were made

The Pale

ULSTER

CONNACHT

DUBLIN

Limerick

LEINSTER

MUNSTER

English plantations in Ireland during Elizabeth I's reign

Henry IV. Shakespeare is said to have written another play with Falstaff in it, *The Merry Wives of Windsor*, because the Queen said she wanted to see 'Sir John in love'.

Shakespeare wrote ten plays about England's history. He got the stories from the chronicles of Ralph Holinshed and Edward Hall, both keen supporters of the Tudors. Hall, in particular, was anxious to show how weak rulers brought about their own downfall by letting great nobles become too powerful. Shakespeare took up this theme in ways which pleased the government; he stressed that obedience to the monarch was essential if disorder, bloodshed and war were to be avoided. One of his most popular plays, *Richard III*, painted the King as a black-hearted villain. This greatly pleased Elizabeth because Richard had been overthrown by her grandfather, Henry VII.

SOURCE 17

This woodcut made in 1581 shows Irish cattle thieves raiding an English plantation in Ireland.

46 Gloriana's people

Plantations in Ireland

The English had conquered a large part of Ireland in medieval times, but by 1500 they only controlled a narrow coastal region round Dublin, known as 'the Pale'. Irish people belonged to clans, like the Scots, and were ruled by chiefs. They farmed mainly by keeping animals, which fed well on Ireland's rich, green pasture. Irish language, laws and customs were different from the English. The religious Reformation further increased the differences between the two peoples because the Irish remained Catholics.

Tudor kings and queens set out to gain greater control of Ireland and so met Irish opposition. Irish chiefs joined in rebellions against Henry VII, and Henry VIII was hated after he closed Irish monasteries. By Elizabeth's reign, there were growing English fears that a Catholic rival such as Spain might make an alliance with Ireland and use the country as a base for attacking England. The English government decided on ruthless measures to crush the Irish. Under a plan nicknamed 'grant and plant', English settlers who were 'granted' land, drove the Irish peasants away and 'planted' themselves on it.

When the Irish fought back they were treated harshly. In the 1570s, a revolt against English rule and the 'plantations' in Munster led to nearly 30,000 deaths from fighting and starvation. When war between England and Spain broke out, in 1588, the Irish appealed to the Spanish to help them drive out the English. King Philip of Spain eventually sent an army to assist an Irish rebellion. To deal with the danger, Elizabeth sent the largest army ever to leave England during Tudor times – 17,000 men, commanded by her new favourite, the Earl of Essex.

Essex was a brave soldier but an unruly and spoilt nobleman. He led his men to defeat in wild, marshy country and then signed a truce with the rebel chief. Elizabeth was furious. She and Essex quarrelled and when Essex staged a hopeless rebellion in London he was captured, sentenced to death and beheaded. The Earl of Mountjoy, who took his place, beat the Irish in 1601 and drove out the Spanish. In future years English plantations multiplied across Ireland. The Irish became outcasts in their own land (**Source 18**).

To the end, Elizabeth never named her successor. But when she died, on 24 March 1603, the next in line was Mary Stuart's son, King James VI of Scotland. A messenger rode north to tell James that he was King of England (**Source 19**).

SOURCE 18

In 1571 the English Governor of Ireland, Sir John Perrot, issued these orders to be obeyed by the people of the Irish province of Munster.

The inhabitants of cities and towns shall wear no mantles (cloaks), shorts, Irish coats, or great shirts, nor allow their hair to grow long … but they are to wear gowns, jerkins, and some civilised garments; and no maid or single woman shall put any great roll or linen cloth upon their heads … [instead] they are to put on hats, caps, French hoods … All bards (minstrels), rhymers and common idle men or women within this province … are to be put in the stocks, there to remain until they shall promise to leave their wicked way of life.

SOURCE 19

Sir Robert Carey was told to carry the news of Elizabeth's death to Scotland. Here he describes his famous ride.

I took horse between nine and ten o'clock; and that night rode to Doncaster. The Friday night I … ordered my deputies to see that the Border be kept quiet. I took horse … so that I might have been with the King at supper time … But I got a great fall by the way … that made me shed much blood. I was forced to ride a soft pace after; so that the King was newly gone to bed by the time I knocked at the gate … I was quickly let in … I kneeled and saluted him by his title … He gave me his hand to kiss, and bade me welcome.

Assessment tasks

A Knowledge and understanding

1 Compare the houses of wealthy Tudor landowners with medieval manor houses. (a) What extra features did the Tudor buildings have? (b) In what ways were they more comfortable to live in?

2 a Why did Tudor governments find it necessary to make laws to deal with the poor?
  b Why do you think better-off people were willing to pay poor rates?
  c Why were 'vagrants' so harshly treated?

3 What do you think was the English government's main motive for 'planting' settlers in Ireland? What were the consequences of this policy, (a) in the short-term, and (b) in the long-term?

B Interpretations and sources

4 Here are two contrasting views of English policy towards Ireland in this period.

> During the reign of Elizabeth I, England succeeded in conquering and colonising large tracts (areas) of Irish land ... Elizabeth's actions in Ireland were disastrous ... Almost half of the Irish people [were] killed ... the entire southern half of Ireland was a barren wilderness, and famine and plague raged in the remainder. Ireland had fallen, but with it [went] England's honour and any hope for future centuries of peace.
> (R. Berleth, 1978)

> [In] the plantation of Ulster ... the Irish were not, as is popularly supposed, driven off the lands wholesale ... The division into counties ... was put into effect. English law took the place of Irish [and] a class of Irish freeholders ... balanced the former power of the chieftain ... The Irish proprietors (landowners) were to be allowed to take as much land as they could develop before [land was given to] English and Scots.
> (A.T.Q. Stewart, 1977)

  a What are the main points of disagreement between these accounts?
  b Can you explain how two historians could come to such different conclusions?
  c Which account do you find the most convincing, and why?

5 From reading Source 18, what do you think was Sir John Perrot's attitude towards the Irish people? Give evidence to support your answer.

6 a What do you learn about Tudor attitudes towards education from Sources 11–14?
  b Do you think these sources are equally reliable?

Gloriana's people

5 The road to Civil War

James I, Charles I and 'Divine Right'

Hark! Hark!
The dogs do bark,
The beggars are coming to town.
Some in rags,
Some in tags,
And some in velvet gown.

This old nursery rhyme is about King James I and his courtiers, riding into England in 1603. As the procession moved south the Scotsmen were astonished by the richness of England compared with their own country. Their 'beggar king', so poor he had to borrow travelling expenses from the English government, was delighted. Never again would he be short of money – or so he thought.

James was the son of Mary Stuart, Queen of Scots, and Lord Darnley (see page 33). He had been King of Scotland since he was a baby. Now the crowns of England and Scotland were united, and from 1603 onwards the two countries were ruled by the same king or queen. James had been unhappy as a child, beaten by his teachers, bullied by nobles and lectured by clergymen. He grew up to be well-educated but timid and cunning. James loved talking and wrote books on various subjects, including witchcraft,

THE STUARTS

James I	1603-1625
Charles I	1625-1649
The Commonwealth	
Charles II	1660-1685
James II	1685-1688
William and Mary	1689-1701
Anne	1701-1714

SOURCE 1

King James I, painted in 1605. In his hat is a jewel called the 'Mirror of Great Britain' which represents the Union of the Crowns of England and Scotland.

> ### SOURCE 2
>
> Sir John Oglander (1585–1655) kept a commonplace book (a sort of diary) in which he wrote down anything that interested him. Here he explains what sort of man he thought James I was.
>
> King James was the most cowardly man I ever knew … to hear of war was death to him. Otherwise he was the best scholar and the wisest prince for general knowledge England ever had … He hated men that spoke ill of others … He had many witty jests … and was very sound in the reformed religion … He loved young men, especially his favourite, the Duke of Buckingham … He was inclined towards peace … and this was his greatest blemish (fault), otherwise he might have been the very best of kings.

monarchy and smoking – which he called 'an ignoble habit'. His favourite sport was hunting, although he rode so slowly that he could rarely keep up with the other riders (**Source 2**).

The crowds who cheered James that spring day in 1603 saw a man who did not like 'playing the king' in public. A Tudor monarch would have waved, smiled and bowed. James was more likely to frown and curse his loyal subjects! But few people cared what he did. They knew James was a Protestant with two sons. Both the Church and the succession to the throne seemed safe after the uncertainties of Elizabeth's reign.

'No bishop, no king'

As James had been brought up a Presbyterian, puritans hoped he would change the Church to their liking. Before he reached London in 1603 puritan clergymen handed him a petititon with a thousand signatures asking for alterations in the Prayer Book and Church services. The King liked talking about religion so in the next year he attended a Church conference at Hampton Court palace.

All went well until one churchman suggested that bishops should have less power. Although he belonged to a Church without bishops, James did not agree. Angrily he told them that those who were against bishops were probably against kings because both were chosen by God. 'No bishop, no king', he shouted, and refused to make any important changes. The only lasting outcome of the conference was a new English translation of the Bible (**Source 3**).

> ### SOURCE 3
>
> Title page of the Authorised Version of the Bible, published with James I's approval in 1611. It took teams of scholars six years to write and is still treasured as one of the greatest works in the English language.

The road to Civil War

James believed monarchs were chosen by God and so had a 'divine right' to rule; they were above the law and must be obeyed (**Source 4**). No other English monarch had ever made such a claim, although some had believed it. James was about to find out that an English king was not free to do as he liked. Since medieval times English kings had ruled with Parliament, asking its advice about laws and taxes. Ordinary people, although they had no votes at elections, expected Parliament to look after their interests and present their grievances to the monarch. Moreover, by James's time some of the richest men in England were MPs. They could not be ignored, especially by a king who was always short of money.

The Gunpowder Plot

Arguments with puritans were followed by more serious trouble with Catholics. When James became king, he promised to change the harsh laws against Catholics. But his ministers did not want him to do this. They persuaded him to keep the laws, particularly the heavy fines on *recusants* (see page 30). The money this raised was used to reward members of the court.

A few disappointed Catholic gentlemen hatched a deadly plot. They would kill the King and his Parliament, seize the royal children and set up a government which would treat Catholics fairly. James, his Lords and Commons, would be blown up with gunpowder when they met for the opening of Parliament in November 1605. The first idea was to dig a tunnel under the hall where the Lords met. Progress was slow so they rented a cellar under the hall instead. They said they wanted to store firewood, but under the wood were 36 barrels of gunpowder.

It seems certain that during the summer Lord Salisbury, James's chief minister, heard about the plot and the gunpowder. He did not tell the King but arranged to 'find out' in an unusual way. In October, Francis Tresham, one of the plotters, wrote a letter to warn his cousin, Lord Monteagle, not to go to the opening of Parliament (**Source 5**). Monteagle showed the letter to Salisbury who took it to the King. James, with God's help so he said, worked out that it meant both the Commons and Lords would be destroyed by an explosion.

Late on 4 November 1605, Guy Fawkes, who had been left behind to light the fuses, was arrested by soldiers hiding in the cellar. The rest of the gang were trapped at Holbeache House in Staffordshire, where there was a fierce fight. Four plotters were killed, two by the same bullet. The survivors were taken to London where they were put on trial, condemned and executed in January 1606. The country rejoiced that God had saved the King. Catholics became even more unpopular. The government ordered that 5 November was to be celebrated each year with bonfires (**Source 6**).

SOURCE 4

On 19 March 1604, at his first meeting with Parliament, James said this.

The state of monarchy is the supremest thing upon Earth: for kings are not only God's assistants upon Earth ... but even by God himself they are called gods in the Scriptures. Kings are also compared to fathers of families; for a king is truly ... father of his people ... As to dispute what God may do is blasphemy (evil speech about God) ... so is it treason in subjects to dispute what a king may do. But just kings will ever be willing to explain what they do ... I will not have my power disputed ... but I shall be willing to rule according to my laws.

SOURCE 5

This is part of Francis Tresham's letter to Lord Monteagle. He was arrested but died in the Tower of London in December 1605, possibly from poison.

My lord, out of the love I bear to some of your friends ... I would advise you as you value your life to make some excuse not to attend this Parliament, for God and man hath decided to punish the wickedness of the time ... I say this Parliament shall receive a terrible blow and yet they shall not say who hurts them. This advice ... may do you good and can do you no harm for the danger is passed as soon as you have burnt the letter.

SOURCE 6

Seventeenth-century drawing showing how Britain was saved from 'Catholic plots'. On the left can be seen the Spanish Armada, in the centre the Pope and his cardinals plotting, and on the right Guy Fawkes in the cellar – but with God watching him.

SOURCE 7

This drawing of Guy Fawkes Day celebrations in the nineteenth century is taken from an 1849 edition of the magazine *Punch*.

52 The road to Civil War

The Petition of Right

Throughout his reign James was short of money. Although Parliament did grant him extra taxes, he raised money in ways which annoyed people. James sold more and more monopolies (see page 41). He also forced men to pay to become *peers* (lords) and knights, and he interfered with trade to get more money from customs duties. All this was condemned as 'illegal' by MPs.

In 1610 James suggested that he should receive a regular income of £200,000 a year instead of all the various taxes and duties. Parliament rejected this suggestion, partly because they thought the figure too high and partly because they thought James wasted too much money on his relatives and friends. The King's chief favourite was the Duke of Buckingham, who had a fortune spent on him over the years.

James died in 1625 and was succeeded by his son, Charles. The new king was a proud, shy man with little sense of humour. He was less intelligent than his father but obstinate and brave. In religion he was a firm supporter of the Church of England. He also took his father's 'Divine Right of Kings' theory very seriously.

The new reign began badly. Just before he died, James had arranged for Charles to marry Henrietta Maria, a French Catholic princess. Henrietta arrived in London with over 100 Catholic servants, including priests. Protestants were horrified. Charles was angry and made her send most of them home. But it was easy for Charles's opponents to say that, with such a wife, the King must be a secret Catholic.

More unpopular than the Queen was the King's best friend, Buckingham, who had been his father's favourite. When war broke out with Catholic Spain it was welcomed by puritans – until Charles put Buckingham in charge of it. The Commons refused to vote enough taxes and, as a result, an attack on the Spanish port of Cadiz failed. Many MPs blamed

SOURCE 8

King Charles I with the symbols of royal power – the crown, orb and sceptre – by his hand.

SOURCE 9

This is the most important part of the Petition of Right.

They do therefore humbly pray your Most Excellent Majesty, that no man be compelled to pay any gift, loan … or such like charge, without the consent of Parliament, and that none be tried or confined, imprisoned or detained without that consent.

The King's answer was:

The King willeth that right be done according to the laws and customs of the realm … that his subjects may have no cause to complain of any wrong.

Buckingham. Charles was already angry with the Commons for not paying for a war they had wanted. Now he got his Court of Star Chamber to imprison without trial any who refused to pay their taxes.

The Commons, led by Sir John Eliot and Sir Thomas Wentworth, drew up a Petition of Right (1628). This requested Charles to stop illegal taxation and imprisonment without trial (**Source 9**). To put pressure on the King they threatened to *impeach* Buckingham. Impeachment was a trial where the Commons acted as accusers and the Lords as judges. Charles reluctantly signed the Petition to save his friend. Soon afterwards the Duke was murdered by John Felton, an army officer. Charles was very upset but Londoners lit bonfires to celebrate and blessed Felton on his way to execution (**Source 10**).

Eleven Years' Tyranny

Next year, when Parliament again asked for changes in the Church, Charles dissolved it and ruled alone for eleven years – the 'Eleven Years' Tyranny' as his opponents called it. The King put Eliot in prison, where he died in 1632, but Wentworth changed sides now that his enemy Buckingham was dead. He was made a minister and given the title Earl of Strafford. Later Charles put him in charge of Ireland.

Outwardly the country seemed calm and peaceful during these years. But quarrels about money went on. Charles raised money in all the ways his father had done. He also thought up some new ideas. For example, Ship Money, a tax paid by ports for the upkeep of the navy, was extended to inland towns. John Hampden, a rich puritan MP, refused to pay. The case went to court where the royal judges decided, by seven to five, that Ship Money was legal. Hampden lost, but the case gave the King's opponents a lot of publicity.

Probably more damaging in the long run was Charles's attitude to the Church. In 1633 he made William Laud Archbishop of Canterbury. Laud detested puritans and ruthlessly punished any vicars who introduced puritan worship into their churches (**Source 12**). Anyone who wrote anything against Laud or the King was also punished. In 1637 William Prynne, Henry Burton and John Bastwicke were sentenced by a Church court to life imprisonment and the loss of their ears for writing such a pamphlet. The London crowd who came to see the men suffer dropped flowers in their path, gave them wine and listened quietly as Prynne gave a sermon while his ears were cut off (**Source 13**).

SOURCE 10

Lord Clarendon (1608–1674) was chief minister to Charles I's son, Charles II. He wrote a *History of the Great Rebellion* covering this period. Clarendon knew Buckingham, and here describes him.

The Duke was an extraordinary person ... never any man ... rose in so short a time to so much greatness, fame and fortune upon no other advantage than the beauty and gracefulness of his person ... [He] promoted almost all of his family, who had no other merit than their relationship with him ... He was of an excellent nature ... generous and bountiful ... It was no more in his nature to be without promotion and titles and wealth than a man can sit in the sun and not get warm.

QUESTIONS

1. What does Charles I's portrait (Source 8) tell you about the way he thought of himself as king?
2. Why do you think Charles's opponents tried to make out he was a secret Catholic?
3. What clues are there in Source 10 which help to explain James I's money problems?
4. In Source 10, what do you think were the writer's feelings about the Duke of Buckingham?

SOURCE 11

The Sovereign of the Seas – one of Charles I's warships, paid for with Ship Money. Launched in 1637, it was the largest ship afloat until 1682. Ten people could get inside the ship's stern lantern.

SOURCE 13

Puritan drawing making fun of Archbishop Laud after the case of Prynne, Burton and Bastwicke (1637).

SOURCE 12

Here Lord Clarendon describes Archbishop Laud.

He intended the discipline of the Church should be felt, as well as spoke of, and that it should apply to the greatest and most splendid of men, as well as to the punishment of smaller offences … Persons of honour and great quality were every day brought before the [Church Court] … upon a scandal in their lives and were prosecuted to their shame … This shame was never forgotten but [they] watched for revenge … Many men turned against bishops who before had no ill-will towards the Church.

James I, Charles I and 'Divine Right'

National Covenant

Feelings were running high against Charles in Scotland as well as England. In 1636 Laud decided that the Scots must use the English Prayer Book in their churches. A majority of Scots were Presbyterian so there was a nationwide protest. Thousands signed a National Covenant (Agreement) to protect their religion. In July 1637, when the Prayer Books came into use, there was uproar. In St Giles's Cathedral, Edinburgh, there was a riot (**Source 14**). At another church a bishop managed to get through a service only by pointing a pair of loaded pistols at the congregation!

There was worse to come. In 1639 the Covenanters, as they were called, gathered an army and invaded England. At last Charles was forced to call Parliament, to pay for an army. To his surprise, many puritan MPs were on the Scots' side. Led by John Pym, the Commons demanded that Charles change his ways and sack Laud and Strafford. Angrily Charles dissolved this 'Short Parliament' after three weeks. But the few poorly-equipped troops he recruited could not hope to take on the Covenanters. Charles had to pay the Scottish army's expenses of £850 a day to stop them advancing any further into

SOURCE 14

Lord Clarendon describes the riot in St Giles's Cathedral, Edinburgh in 1637.

On the Sunday morning appointed for the work ... the dean began to read the prayers from the Prayer Book, which no sooner he started, but a noise and clamour was raised throughout the church, that no words could be heard distinctly, and than a shower of stones and sticks were thrown at the dean's head ... The magistrates of the city [managed] to drive the rudest of those who made the disturbance out of the church ... but they continued their noise, broke the windows and tried to break down the doors ... with bitter curses against bishops.

SOURCE 15

Execution of the Earl of Strafford on Tower Hill. This drawing was made soon afterwards.

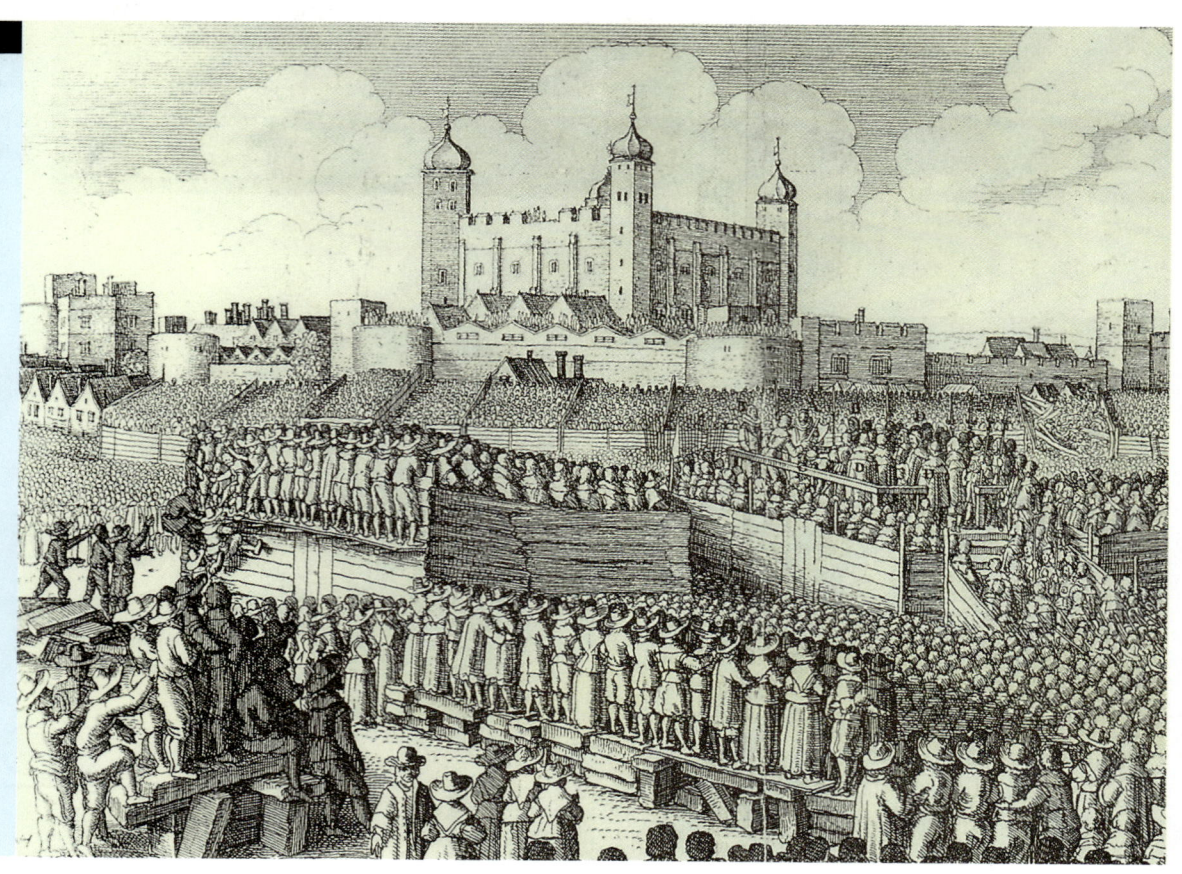

England. After nine months he had no money left. He was completely at the mercy of the next Parliament he had to call, in 1641.

The so-called 'Long Parliament' – it sat for 13 years – arrested Laud and put him on trial. He was condemned to death, although the sentence was not carried out until 1645. Strafford was accused of plotting to bring troops from Ireland to put down the King's opponents. In the end he was declared guilty of treason. For a time Charles wondered whether to save his minister by using force to arrest Pym and his friends. But when he heard that they were prepared to impeach the Queen for 'Catholic plots' he gave way. Strafford was beheaded in front of a vast crowd on Tower Hill, London, in May 1641.

Grand Remonstrance and War

The Long Parliament closed Church courts and the court of Star Chamber. It abolished all the King's illegal taxes and duties. A Triennial Bill was passed making it necessary, in future, to call Parliament at least every three years. It was a complete surrender on the part of the King.

Suddenly the situation changed dramatically. A serious rebellion broke out in Ireland where Catholics attacked Protestant settlers (**Source 16**). Once again Charles asked Parliament for an army, to crush this rising. Pym and his supporters knew they were in great danger; if the King got an army he would use it to crush them first! They decided to make a direct appeal to the people. A docu-

Driuinge Men women & children by hund: reds vpon Briges & casting them into Riuers, who drowned not were killed with poles & shot with muskets.

SOURCE 16

Irish Catholics killing Protestant settlers in Ireland, 1641. This drawing was published in England where it caused an outcry against the Irish.

> **QUESTIONS**
>
> 1. In Source 13, what is Archbishop Laud about to eat? Why would such a drawing have made him angry?
> 2. How can you tell from Source 14 that the riot was planned in advance?
> 3. Can you think of two reasons why the execution of an important person (as in Source 15) was made such a public spectacle?
> 4. Why might Source 16 have been exaggerated?

SOURCE 17

Sir Ralph Verney (1611–1696) was a member of the Long Parliament. He was present when the King entered the Commons' chamber and he wrote down what happened in a notebook on his knee.

Tuesday, January 4 ... The five gentlemen which were to be accused came into the House, and there was information that they should be taken away by force ... A little after, the King came with all his guard ... He told us he would not break our privileges, but treason had no privilege ... He asked the Speaker if the five were present ... The Speaker fell on his knees and said he had neither eyes, nor tongue, to see or say anything but what they (the MPs) commanded him. Then the King told him he thought his own eyes were good and then said, his birds were flown.

SOURCE 18

Nottingham Castle, where Charles I began his Civil War campaign.

---

ment called the Grand Remonstance was produced, listing all the things Charles was said to have done wrong during his reign. It also suggested less power for bishops and changes in church services to suit puritans.

The Grand Remonstance was the turning point on the road to war. People of those times usually supported the monarchy. They saw it as a God-given form of government, and even those who disliked Charles were not against monarchy as such. To many MPs, the Grand Remonstance went too far by aiming to alter the monarchy and the Church. In a tense debate on 22 November 1641, men drew their swords and tore at each other's clothes and hair. The Grand Remonstance was passed, but only just – by 159 votes to 148. Until that night most of the Commons had been against the King. Now nearly half were for him.

In his excitement the King acted foolishly. On the Queen's advice, he went to Parliament to arrest five of the ringleaders, including Pym. Charles entered the Commons' chamber on 4 January 1642 with armed soldiers **(Source 17)**. The five MPs had been warned and were not there. Next day they paraded through the streets guarded by the London Trained Bands (part-time soldiers). After such open defiance, Charles no longer felt safe in his own capital. He left London to recruit an army. His Parliamentary opponents did the same. On 22 August 1642 the King raised his standard (flag) at Nottingham as a sign of war. A few days later a high wind blew it down. The English Civil war had begun.

Assessment tasks

A Knowledge and understanding

1 Make a timeline of important dates leading up to the outbreak of the Civil War in 1642. Divide events into two columns, one headed *political* and the other *religious*. Include not just events in particular years but also things that happened over longer periods of time.

2 Here are some possible causes of the Civil War. Add more if you wish.

- Disputes about how religious services should be conducted.
- Charles I's eleven years' rule without Parliament.
- The Irish rebellion of 1641.
- King Charles's belief in the 'Divine Right of Kings'.
- The attempt to force the English Prayer Book on Scotland.
- Charles's attempt to arrest the five MPs.
- The King raising taxes without Parliament's permission.

  a Re-arrange these causes in what you consider to be their order of importance.
  b Divide them into (i) short-term, and (ii) long-term causes.

3 Most MPs and many of King Charles's subjects thought he was in the wrong when he entered the Commons' chamber with soldiers in January 1642. Can you explain (a) why they took this view, and (b) why Charles had a different attitude?

B Interpretations and sources

4 Here are two accounts by twentieth-century historians of the punishment of Prynne, Burton and Bastwicke.

> The speakers (the three prisoners), with their heads through the pillory, spoke much of their faith in Jesus … [and] in the ancient liberties of England. In the great crowd below many wept aloud and … were moved to honest English anger at the cruelty inflicted on the brave [men]. When the hangman sawed off Prynne's ears a yell arose to which Charles I should have listened.
> (G.M. Trevelyan, 1904)

> 'The intention of these men', Laud declared justly at their trial, 'was to raise a sedition (to overthrow the government) for they are … revolutionaries against the state …' On June 30, 1637, a hot, bright day, the victims were led out to suffer … Sympathetic crowds had gathered to watch … The sufferers stood in their pulpits (the pillory) for two hours … and had plenty to preach, Prynne speaking loudest and longest … The Archbishop's annoyance when he heard of the demonstration was mixed with anxiety.
> (C.V. Wedgewood, 1955)

Both accounts are biased, in different directions. Can you detect the bias in each?

5 Compare the different views of the Gunpowder Plot pictured in Sources 6 and 7. What changes in attitudes, between the seventeenth and nineteenth centuries, do they show towards (i) the Plot, (ii) the Pope, and (iii) religion in general?

6 a What does Source 2 tell us about how a king in those days was expected to behave?
  b Are different things expected of rulers or governments today? Give reasons for your answer.

6 Divided by the sword

Civil War and the rule of Cromwell

Although the Civil War was between King and Parliament, half the House of Commons and a majority of the Lords fought for the King. The country was split geographically. The wealthier regions of the South and East Anglia were for Parliament. The poorer areas of the North and West fought for the King. Most towns supported Parliament, some because they were run by puritans, others because they hated the King's taxes.

Division of England between Cavaliers and Roundheads on the outbreak of the Civil War, 1642

Consequently the Parliamentary side was the wealthier of the two. The King had trouble throughout the war paying for soldiers, weapons and equipment.

Cavaliers and Roundheads

The nicknames of the two sides – Cavaliers and Roundheads – came from insults they gave each other. Supporters of Parliament said the royalists were like the brutal Spanish *cabbaleros* (cavaliers, or horsemen) who had massacred Protestants in Holland in the time of Elizabeth I. The London apprentices who rioted against King Charles in 1642 had short haircuts, so their opponents called them Roundheads.

The war was mainly between gentlemen landowners over how the country should be governed. Ordinary folk, unless they were puritans, were not particularly interested. A labourer went to war on the side of his lord or local squire, changed sides if his lord changed sides, and sometimes joined the enemy army if captured. Soldiers were unpopular with civilians. They had no barracks in those days so they were lodged, rent-free, with families. Drunken troops often damaged houses, stole property and assaulted both men and women.

Women shared the dangers and discomforts of the war. During sieges they made bullets, dug trenches and repaired town walls. After battles they fed and nursed the wounded and dying. Wives of gentlemen sometimes defended their mansions when their husbands were away. The elderly Lady Stafford commanded the defenders of Stafford Castle against the Roundheads and then managed to escape when the castle was captured. The Queen herself was in danger whilst with the royal army. She once crouched in a ditch as cannonballs flew overhead.

It was a war which divided families and friends (**Source 1**). In 1643 a royalist soldier wrote to his Roundhead brother, 'Though I am tooth and nail for the King's cause and shall be to the death … yet, sweet brother, let this not cause a difference of my true love for you'. Some who fought were less sure of the rightness of their cause and had very mixed feelings about the war (**Source 2**).

From Edgehill to Nantwich

The King's first move was against London, the headquarters of Parliament. Roundhead troops barred his way at Edgehill in Warwickshire, where the first major battle was fought (23 October 1642). The King's nephew, Prince Rupert, commanded the royal cavalry. Although young, he was an experienced soldier who had

SOURCE 1

Sir William Waller, a Roundhead general, wrote this letter to his old friend, Sir Ralph Hopton, who was a general in the King's army. A few weeks later Hopton defeated Waller in a battle near Bath.

The happiness I have enjoyed in your friendship makes me sad when I look upon the present distance between us … But I must be true to the cause wherein I serve … That great God … knows with what a sad heart I go upon this service, and with what a perfect hatred I detest this war without an enemy … We are both set upon a stage and must act those parts given us in this tragedy. Let us do it with honour, and without personal dislike …

Your affectionate friend and faithful servant,
Wm. Waller
Bath, 16 June 1643

SOURCE 2

Edmund Verney was the King's standard-bearer at the battle of Edgehill (1642) where he was killed. A few weeks earlier he had made these remarks to a friend.

I do not like the quarrel, and do heartily wish that the King would consent to what they desire … My only concern now is to follow my master. I have served him for thirty years, and will not … desert him; but I choose rather to lose my life (which I am sure I shall do) than defend things which are against my conscience … For I will speak frankly with you, I have no liking for the Bishops, for whom this quarrel is being fought.

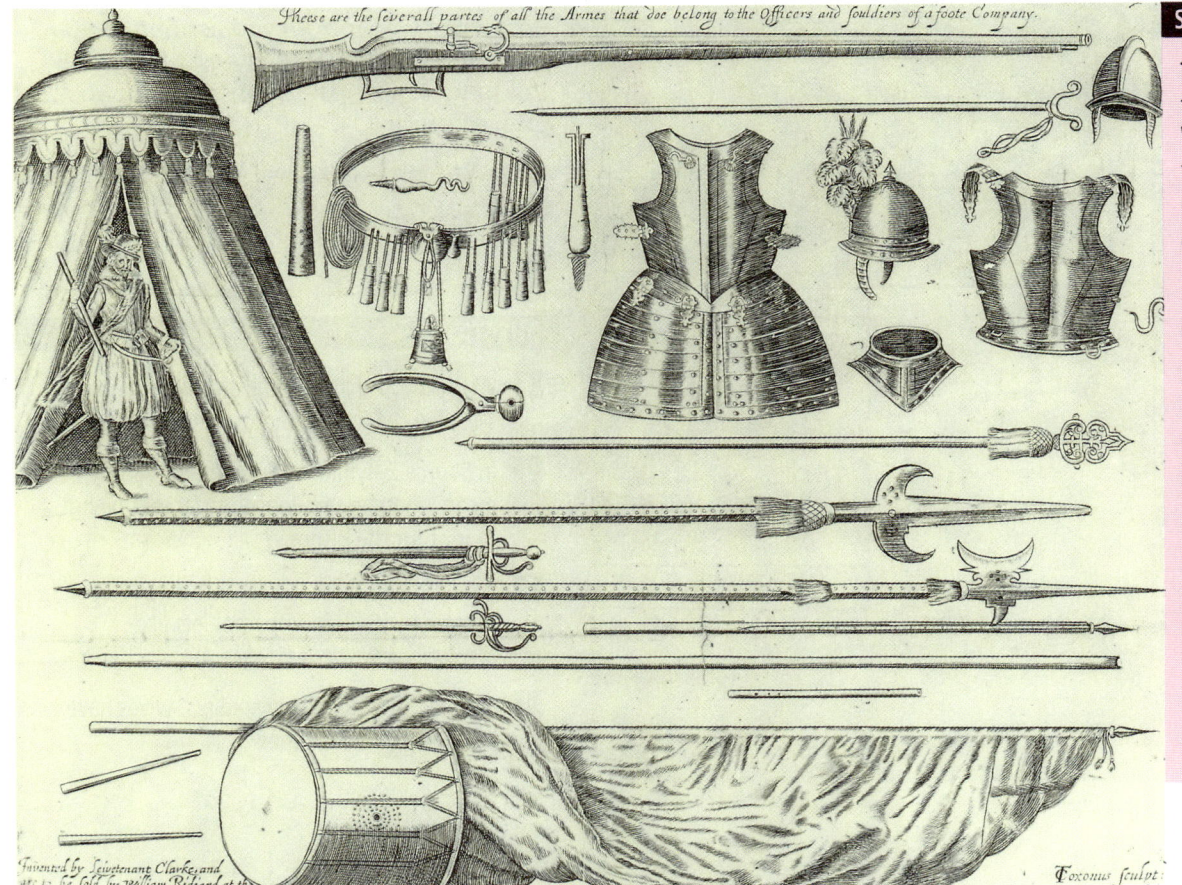

SOURCE 3

This drawing, made at the time of the Civil War, shows some of the weapons and equipment used. *From the top:* musket and rest for the barrel, leather baldrick (belt) with containers of powder and a bag of bullets, body armour and helmets, and a selection of halberds (combined spear and battle-axe). The drum and flag were used to give signals during the heat of a battle.

SOURCE 4

A Royalist pamphlet, *Mercurious Rusticus* (Country News), tells of horrors committed by Roundheads. At the bottom, men are shown fighting with pikes (weapons like spears) at the battle of Edgehill.

fought in European wars.

Rupert led a furious charge which broke the left wing of the Roundhead forces. His men then galloped for miles before he could stop them. Meanwhile, the infantry (foot-soldiers) on each side fought until exhausted. At one time the King himself was in danger; his standard (flag) was captured and sixty of his bodyguard killed. Only darkness stopped the fighting. It was a drawn battle but Charles had failed to take London.

Three royal armies tried to capture the capital in 1643. Each was held up by Roundhead towns barring their advance. Charles decided to attack Gloucester, which was holding out for Parliament, but he was driven off by troops which had marched from London (**Source 5**). During the following winter both sides looked for outside help. Parliament got the Scots to join them by promising to set up a presbyterian church in England after the war. Charles signed a truce with the Catholic

SOURCE 5

This letter was written in 1643 by a wife to her husband away at the war. It is not known whether he ever received it.

Most dear and loving husband, [I hope] you are in good health … My little Willie have been sick this fortnight. I pray you to come home if you can come safely. I do marvel (am surprised) that I cannot hear from you as well as other neighbours do. I do desire to hear from you as soon as you can. I thought you would never leave me this long … so I rest ever praying for your safe return,

Your loving wife,
Susan Rodway

QUESTIONS

1. Why do you think Sir William Waller (Source 1) called it a 'war without an enemy'?
2. In Source 2, what did Sir Edmund Verney mean when he said that the war was being fought for the bishops?
3. What do you think the royalists hoped to achieve by publishing pamphlets like *Mercurious Rusticus* (Source 4)?
4. Why might letters from soldiers' wives have been rare in those times?

rebels in Ireland (see page 57). This freed an Irish Protestant army to come to England to fight for him.

Parliament got much the better deal. A well-trained Scottish army crossed the border, led by David Leslie, another soldier who had fought in European wars. This army threatened the royal hold on the North. The Irish troops, on the other hand, were beaten easily by Sir Thomas Fairfax at Nantwich in Cheshire (January 1644). Afterwards, thousands of the Irish joined the Roundheads!

Marston Moor

On Parliament's side, soldiers began to take over the leadership from civilians. Pym had died in 1643 and generals such as Fairfax and Cromwell became more powerful. Oliver Cromwell was a gentleman-farmer and MP from Huntingdonshire. In religion, he agreed with a group called the Independents who wanted people to be free to worship as they wished. At the start of the war Cromwell formed a cavalry troop. He taught his men to advance at a trot which was easier to control than Rupert's charges. It was Rupert who gave them the nickname 'Ironsides' when he saw their steady discipline in battle.

In the summer of 1644 Charles's commander in the North, the Duke of Newcastle, was trapped in York by the armies of Fairfax and Leslie. Rupert raced to the rescue, saved the city and challenged the Roundheads to battle on nearby Marston Moor (2 July 1644). As it took some hours for all the troops to assemble, Rupert and Newcastle assumed there would be no fighting that day. The Duke went to his coach and lit his pipe; Rupert started to eat his supper. Suddenly, with only an hour of daylight left, Cromwell saw a chance to get his forces across a ditch which might be a serious obstacle next day.

This advance sparked off a full-scale battle. Rupert had not reached his cavalry when the Ironsides struck and scattered them, after a fierce struggle. The royal infantry fought bravely until broken by Cromwell's charges. The Whitecoats, a royalist regiment, fought to the last in a wood. About midnight Fairfax tried to stop the killing, waving his sword and shouting to his men 'Save your countrymen'. Only about thirty Whitecoats survived to surrender. Rupert escaped from the moor alone, leaving 'Boy', his poodle, dead. The North was lost to the King.

The New Model Army

During the winter Parliament formed England's first *standing* (permanent) army. It was called the New Model and its 22,000 men were well equipped, highly trained and well paid. Its commander was Fairfax and its cavalry was led by Cromwell. Discipline was strict: men were whipped for swearing and the penalty for threatening an officer was death. Every man was

SOURCE 6

Oliver Cromwell. He was descended from a Welshman, Morgan Williams, who had married a sister of Thomas Cromwell (see page 20) and changed his name to hers.

Civil War and the rule of Cromwell

taught to believe that he was fighting for God.

When the King faced this new army at Naseby in Northamptonshire (14 June 1645) he was short of supplies and outnumbered by two to one. Rupert was anxious not to be surprised this time so he attacked first. But again his men charged too fast and too far. Cromwell's horsemen were able to beat the royalist infantry before the Prince returned. Charles wanted to die fighting, but an officer grabbed the reins of his horse and led him away. Naseby was the last major battle. The King had lost the war.

It was May 1646 before the final royalist stronghold surrendered. Charles did not wish to fall into the hands of Parliament so he gave himself up to the Scots. But when he refused to help them establish the presbyterian religion in England they handed him over to Parliament in return for money to pay their troops. It seemed a great Roundhead victory but behind the scenes there were disagreements. Parliament was determined to set up the presbyterian church it had promised the Scots. But many of its soldiers were Independents who wanted freedom of worship. They had not risked their lives to see one kind of religious discipline replaced by another.

The New Model was not an ordinary army. Its soldiers, who were very religious, spent their time in prayer, discussion and debate. There were some in its ranks who wanted to change the government as well as the Church. These 'Levellers' suggested doing away with the monarchy and the House of Lords, holding elections to Parliament every two years and giving most men over 21 the right to vote (Source 8). Cromwell rejected such ideas. He wanted religious, not political change. Later, in 1649, he crushed a Leveller mutiny in the army and executed some of the ringleaders.

With the fighting over, Parliament ordered the army to disband but refused to pay wages owed to the soldiers. The New Model's response was to seize the King and offer him their own terms. He could reign again, with the Church of England as state church, provided he allowed other religious groups freedom of worship. Charles, who looked upon the army leaders as enemies of God, rejected the offer and escaped to the Isle of Wight (1647) where he had secret meetings with the Scots. He promised to set up a presby-

SOURCE 7

The battle of Naseby, seen from the Roundhead side. The left wing commanded by Ireton (Cromwell's son-in-law) faces Prince Rupert's cavalry. In the centre the King rides alone. On the right Cromwell faces the Royalist cavalry.

SOURCE 8

Here are some of the Levellers' ideas, which they published in a document called *The Agreement of the People*.

That the vote be given to all housekeepers of twenty-one who have not aided the King or impeded (obstructed) the Army [but not] to persons on alms (receiving poor relief), wage-earners and servants ...
That matters of religion and God's worship are not given to us by human power ... [so we must follow] what our consciences tell us to be the mind of God ...
That the impressing (forcing) of us to serve in wars is against our freedom ...
That in all laws every person must obey alike

Divided by the sword

terian church in England for a trial period of three years if they would help him defeat Parliament.

The resulting Second Civil War did not last long. In August 1648 Cromwell destroyed the Scots army at Preston. Then he and Fairfax put down royalist risings in Kent, Essex and Wales. The New Model now decided to settle once and for all with both Parliament and the King. In December, musketeers led by Colonel Pride entered the House of Commons, arrested 41 MPs suspected of plotting with the King and expelled 96 others. Only a 'Rump', or remnant, of the original Long Parliament now remained. For the next eleven years the Army was the real power in England.

Trial and execution

As far as the soldiers were concerned, God had already passed sentence on Charles in battle. His defeats were a sign that God was against him. Furthermore, he was a traitor to have plotted with the Scots and invited them into England. On 20 January 1649, a 'High Court of Justice' was set up to try him. The Army found 135 judges prepared to take part. Fifty-nine of these signed Charles's death warrant.

The trial took place in Westminster Hall, London. Charles was at his best during his last days. He faced his judges calmly and

SOURCE 9

The trial of Charles I in Westminster Hall.

SOURCE 10

The death warrant of Charles I. Of those who signed, 46 were alive when Charles II restored the monarchy in 1660. Many fled the country, but nine were hanged, drawn and quartered. The bodies of Cromwell and his son-in-law, Ireton, were dug up, hanged and beheaded.

Civil War and the rule of Cromwell **65**

told them, 'The King cannot be tried'. Certainly it was not legal to try the King for treason because this was a crime against the monarch! So Charles refused to answer any of the charges. After several days of argument, the court sentenced 'The said Charles Stuart, as a Tyrant, Traitor and Murderer and public enemy', to be put to death, 'by the severing of his head from his body'.

On 30 January 1649 Charles went bravely to his death on a scaffold set up in Whitehall, London. It was a bitterly cold day with ice floating on the Thames and the ground white with frost and snow. The executioner wore a mask and false beard as a disguise. Charles made a short speech (**Source 11**), laid his head on the block and raised his arm as a signal to the axeman. A great groan went up from the crowd as his head was cut off with one blow.

SOURCE 11

King's last speech could not be heard by the crowd, but it was taken down by clerks on the scaffold. John Rushworth, who was probably present at the execution, published this version in 1701.

Truly I desire their (the people's) liberty and freedom as much as anybody ...; but I must tell you that their ... liberty and freedom consists in having a government [and] those laws by which their life and their goods may be most their own. It is not for having a share in government ... that is nothing to do with them. A subject and a sovereign are clear different things ... If I would have given way ... I needed not have come here ... I am a martyr of the people.

SOURCE 12

Over the years Cromwell had been angered by stories of Catholic murders of Protestants in Ireland. When he arrived in the country he behaved with great cruelty, as this letter from him to the Commons, dated 17 September 1649, shows.

And, indeed, I forbade them (the soldiers) to spare any that were in arms in the town (Drogheda), and, I think, that night they put to the sword (killed) about 2000 men ... One hundred others were in St. Peter's church ... These being summoned to yield ... refused, whereupon I ordered St. Peter's church to be set on fire where one of them was heard to say in the midst of the flames, 'God damn me, God confound me: I burn, I burn ...' This is the righteous judgement of God upon these barbarous wretches.

Commonwealth and Protectorate

England, Wales, Scotland and Ireland were now declared a Commonwealth – that is, a republic (a state without a monarch). The Irish and Scots had not been asked whether they wanted this union and both objected. Ireland was still in a state of rebellion (see page 57). In the autumn of 1649 this was put down by Cromwell in a brutal, whirlwind campaign in which he executed prisoners (**Source 12**).

Meanwhile the Scots were furious when the Army prevented a presbyterian church being established in England. They invited the dead King's son to reign as Charles II. Cromwell invaded Scotland and defeated the Scots at Dunbar (3 September 1650). The Scots, however, went on fighting and, in January 1651, crowned Charles II king. In August, while Cromwell was still in Scotland, Charles advanced south with 10,000 men, hoping to rouse royalists in England. Cromwell followed him to Worcester, where the royal army was destroyed in a fierce street battle (3 September 1651). Charles escaped abroad after many adventures, including hiding in an oak tree from Roundhead soldiers.

At first the Commonwealth was ruled by the 'Rump' of Parliament. Then the Army began to complain, claiming its members were selfish and dishonest. In April 1653 Cromwell dissolved what was left of Parliament, driving its members out with musketeers. This ended legal government in England – and set Cromwell and the New Model a problem they never solved. Cromwell was made Lord Protector, ruling with the help of a Council of State. He would have liked to hold elections but knew that most of the gentry would vote to abolish army rule. This Cromwell would never allow. He was sure that God had meant the Army to rule; why else would He have let them win the war?

Cromwell experimented with several 'parliaments' picked by the Army. He quarrelled with all of them. In 1655–56 the country was divided into eleven districts, each ruled by a Major General. Such mili-

SOURCE 13

Cromwell dissolves the Rump Parliament, April 1653. The artist was Dutch (notice the words 'This House is to Let' in Dutch as well as English). The MPs are leading out an owl, a symbol of wisdom, so the artist probably disagreed with what Cromwell had done.

tary rule turned everyone against the Army. Gentlemen were outraged that 'tradesmen and labourers' were ruling the counties, for many of the army officers were from poor backgrounds (**Source 14**). The lives of the people were made a misery by men who closed theatres and race-meetings, banned Christmas celebrations and fined people for swearing.

Cromwell was successful in foreign wars. The New Model Army beat the Spanish in a land battle (1658) and a British fleet seized Spanish treasure ships and captured Jamaica in the West Indies. Cromwell was feared and respected throughout Europe. But at home people were tired of military rule and the heavy taxes needed to pay for the New Model Army and a large navy. Only Cromwell's great reputation and powerful personality kept things going.

The Restoration, 1660

Cromwell became a king in all but name. When he died, on 3 September 1658 – the anniversary of his victories at Dunbar and Worcester – his son, Richard, became Lord Protector. But 'Tumbledown Dick', as he

SOURCE 14

These remarks come from the writings of Sir John Oglander, a royalist. He disliked being ruled by committees of ordinary tradesmen and farmers.

I believe such times were never before seen in England, when the gentry were made slaves to the common people and in their power, not only to abuse but plunder any gentleman ... We have here a thing called a committee, which over-ruled Deputy Lieutenants and also Justices of the Peace ... Ringwood of Newport, the pedlar, Maynard, the apothecary (shopkeeper), Matthews the Baker, Wavell and Legge, farmers ... These ruled the whole island (Isle of Wight) and did whatsoever they thought good in their own eyes.

SOURCE 15

Charles II, on the white horse, rides in procession to Westminster in 1661.

QUESTIONS

1. How do you think the Levellers got their name?
2. Why did the King's executioner disguise himself?
3. Can you think of a reason why many inns are called *The Royal Oak*?
4. What do you imagine Charles II thought of some of the people who greeted him when he entered London (Source 16)?

SOURCE 16

Lord Clarendon (1608–74) was a minister to both Charles I and II. This account of Charles II's arrival in England in 1660 comes from his *History of the Great Rebellion*.

On Monday he went to Rochester; and the next day, being ... his birthday, he entered London ... The King rode in a crowd from the bridge to Temple-bar; all the companies (guilds) of the city ... giving loud thanks to God for his majesty's presence. And he no sooner came to Whitehall, but the two houses of parliament solemnly cast themselves at his feet, with all vows (promises) of affection and fidelity (loyalty) to the world's end ... His majesty said smilingly ... he thought it had been his own fault that he had been absent so long; for he saw nobody that did not protest he had ever wished for his return.

was called, had never been a soldier and relied on civilian advisers. The Army did not like him and, after only nine months, he was forced to resign.

The army generals recalled the Rump Parliament, hoping it would make them more popular. However the Rump wanted to disband the Army so it was again dissolved. The country was now in disorder, with the army leaders undecided what to do. General George Monck's army, stationed in Scotland, marched south to restore order. It was cheered on its way by crowds chanting for 'free elections'. In London, Monck allowed the Long Parliament to re-assemble.

England now had a legal government. It seemed that all it needed was a king. Charles II was invited to take the Crown, provided he ruled with Parliament. Charles agreed, and sailed from Holland where he had been living in exile. On 29 May 1660 he entered London in triumph (**Source 16**). This Restoration of the monarchy ended what is known as the *Interregnum* – Latin for a gap or interval between the reigns of two kings. The New Model Army was disbanded, apart from one regiment (now the Coldstream Guards) which joined the new royal army.

Assessment tasks

A Knowledge and understanding

1. Make your own list of reasons why Parliament won the Civil War. Which do you think was the most important single reason, and why?

2. 'I needed not have come here', said King Charles on the scaffold. What evidence is there that his execution was no one's fault but his own?

3. Here are two views of Oliver Cromwell from men who knew him. The first comes from the poet, John Milton, who served in the Commonwealth government. The second was written in the 1660s by Lord Clarendon, chief minister to Charles II.

   > You ... the author of liberty ...have outstripped not only the achievements of our kings, but even the legends of our heroes ... You have taken upon yourself ... to rule three powerful nations ... to lead their peoples to a better standard of morality and discipline.

   > To reduce three nations, which perfectly hated him, to obedience ... was a prodigious (great) achievement ... But his greatness at home was but a shadow of the glory he had abroad. It was hard to discover which feared him most, France, Spain or the Low Countries (now Holland and Belgium) ... He will be looked upon by posterity (people to come) as a brave, bad man.

   Which of these do you think is nearer the truth, and why?

B Interpretations and sources

4. Here are two modern accounts of the end of the battle of Marston Moor.

   > Newcastle's Whitecoats in the centre – local men fighting passionately for their own cause on their own home ground – still struggled on ... So it was that, refusing all offers of quarter (mercy), they died where they stood, scarcely thirty of them surviving ... Cromwell's victorious cavalry [pursued] Goring's horse (cavalry) almost to York itself ... The allied armies settled down to a Psalm of thanksgiving.
   > (Antonia Fraser, 1973)

   > The Whitecoat musketeers had long ago fired off all their shot ... Cromwell at last unleashed his puritan troopers, and they were changed from iron discipline to passionate cruelty. Roundhead cavalry thundered across the field after defeated Royalists, cutting them down left and right like helpless animals ... The three-mile road to York was lined with slain (dead bodies). The streets of York were choked with screaming men left untended in rows in the open air ... After the killing was over, the blood-stained and hungry Roundhead army joined with the Scots in singing King David's Psalm of victory.
   > (J. Barbary, 1977)

   How are the actions of Cromwell and the Roundheads described differently in these two accounts? What do these differences tell you about each writer's views?

5. Describe the different attitudes towards war of Sir William Waller, Sir Edmund Verney and Susan Rodway (Sources 1, 2 and 5). How do they help us to understand the unhappiness that the war caused?

6. What do the sources in this chapter tell you about the different attitudes towards God and religion at that time?

7 Ideas and discoveries

Arts and sciences in the seventeenth century

As he sailed back to England in 1660, King Charles II (**Source 1**) told his companions of his escape from the Roundheads after the battle of Worcester. One of his listeners, Samuel Pepys, wrote down what the King said in his diary. Pepys kept his diary secret by using a form of shorthand called *tachygraphy* (fast-writing). He was a government official who knew many important people. When his diary was decoded in 1822, it revealed a lot about Charles II and his times.

The world of Samuel Pepys

Pepys worked for the Navy in London. He lived through many famous events, including a war with Holland and the last great attack of the plague in 1665. Another dramatic event happened in the following year. On 2 September 1666, Pepys was awakened with news of a dreadful fire. It had started in a baker's shop in Pudding Lane, near London Bridge, and spread quickly. Pepys wrote an account of the Great Fire in his diary. He told of warehouses full of oil, tar and brandy burning fiercely, and pigeons dropping to the ground with burnt wings. As night fell on the first day, he saw 'The churches, houses and all ... one entire arch of fire'.

The Fire of London raged for four days, destroying 13,000 houses as well as churches and other public buildings. On 5 September, Pepys went to Moorfields where many of the homeless were camp-

SOURCE 1

Bishop Gilbert Burnet knew Charles II and disapproved of his love of pleasure. Here he describes another side of the King's character.

He had a great compass of knowledge, tho' he was never capable of much study. He understood Mechanics and Physics; and was a good Chemist ... He understood navigation well ... He was an everlasting talker. He told his stories with a good grace: but told them too often. He had a very ill opinion of men and women ... He thought nobody did serve him out of love ... and loved others as little as he thought they loved him.

SOURCE 2

Samuel Pepys, painted in 1666. He was a keen musician, and is holding the manuscript of a song he wrote called 'Beauty Retire'.

70 Ideas and discoveries

SOURCE 3

The Great Fire of 1666, viewed from the south bank of the Thames. Old St Paul's Cathedral can be seen burning in the centre of the drawing.

ing. His feet, he wrote, 'were ready to burn among the hot coals of the streets'. Two days later he visited the ruins of old St. Paul's Cathedral, 'a miserable sight ... with the roof fallen' **(Source 4)**. He reported that Londoners were saying, 'there is a plot in it and that the French have done it'. This was not true; the fire was accidental, probably started by an over-heated oven.

After the Great Fire, nearly sixty new churches were built by Sir Christopher Wren (1632–1723). Wren's most famous building was the new St. Paul's Cathedral

SOURCE 4

Pepys was too busy to write each day while the Fire of London was raging. He made scribbled shorthand notes and wrote a full account later. Here is part of the story of the first day, 2 September 1666.

As soon as I had dined, I walked through the City, the streets (were) full of people and horses and carts ... removing goods from one burned house to another ... I met with the King and the Duke of York in their Barge ... Their order was to pull down houses ... The river was full of boats taking goods, and goods swimming in the water ... We went as near the fire as we could ... with one's face in the wind you were almost burned with a shower of Firedrops.

SOURCE 5

St Paul's Cathedral – Sir Christopher Wren's most famous building. It was built on wet sand and gravel. When this dried out during the eighteenth century the foundations began to give way and had to be repaired. During the Second World War a bomb hit the cathedral but failed to explode.

QUESTIONS

1. Can you think of any reason why Charles II might have 'had a very ill opinion of men and women' (Source 1)?
2. What factors would have made the Great Fire of 1666 harder to deal with than a similar fire today?
3. During the Great Fire, why do you think the King was advising people to 'pull down houses' (Source 4)?
4. In what ways might the Great Fire have had good effects?

Arts and sciences in the seventeenth century

(**Source 5**). Its style is called *Palladian*, after the work of Andreas Palladio, an Italian architect who copied ancient Roman designs. St Paul's took thirty years to build and is the only Palladian cathedral in Britain.

The Royal Society

Both Wren and Pepys were members of the Royal Society, a club for men who were interested in science. The club met each week to listen to talks or watch experiments. It was founded in 1662 in Wren's rooms at Gresham College in London, and the King allowed it to use the title 'Royal'. Members paid 1 shilling (5p) a week subscription and, as well as weekly meetings, had what Pepys called 'pretty suppers'. Pepys was not a scientist but his work meant that he could give the Society useful information about tides, navigation and ships (**Source 6**).

At Society meetings doctors conducted experiments with animals, scientists explained the workings of the universe and sailors gave talks about their voyages. Members liked to discover new facts and test old beliefs. For centuries it had been believed that a spider would never leave a circle made of powdered horn. The members put a spider in such a circle and it walked out! Robert Hooke, a famous scientist, showed them the wonders he had seen with his microscope, a new invention from Holland (**Source 7**).

When Prince Rupert, in command of a royal fleet, sailed to fight the Dutch off the African coast, the Royal Society asked him if he could measure the depth of the ocean in his spare time. Rupert himself was a member of the Society and a keen scientist. He invented a new kind of gunpowder, navigational instruments and a pistol which worked like a machine gun.

The Royal Society gave scientists a chance to meet and discuss their discoveries. It encouraged people to ask questions about the world around them. Perhaps most important of all, it helped put science in the news. Today, to be a Fellow of the Royal Society (FRS) is a high honour for a scientist.

Milton and Dryden

Even during the plague Pepys managed to enjoy himself. One of his favourite pastimes was watching plays. Theatres had re-opened in 1660 after being closed by the puritans (see Chapter 6). Pepys particularly liked the new fashion of letting women act on stage instead of their parts being played by boys. The most famous actress of the time was Nell Gwynne, one of the King's favourites. Nell was very cheeky; she called the King 'Charles III' because she had two other boy-friends called Charles!

One famous playwright, John Dryden, had been a friend of Pepys since they were students at Cambridge University. Dryden's plays were so successful that he was able to lend the King money. Dryden also wrote poems, some about great events like the Dutch War and the Fire of London (**Source 8**). In 1677 he set John Milton's long poem, *Paradise Lost*, to music. Milton was a strong supporter of Parliament. In 1649 he had written a pamphlet defending

---

SOURCE 6

Pepys was a keen member of the Royal Society and became its President in 1687. These diary entries describe three similar experiments carried out at meetings of the Society.

16 May 1664 ... Went to see an experiment of killing a dog by letting opium into his hind leg ... The dog did presently fall asleep and so lay until we cut him up.

14 November 1666 ... Tonight there was a pretty experiment, of the blood of one dog let out, till he died, into the body of another on one side, while all his own run out on the other side ... The other did very well, and likely to do well ... This did give occasion to many pretty wishes, as of the blood of a Quaker (a Noncomformist) to be let into an Archbishop.

21 November 1667 ... The College (the Royal Society) have hired for 20 shillings (£1) ... a man that is a little frantic ... to have some of the blood of a sheep let into his body.

SOURCE 7

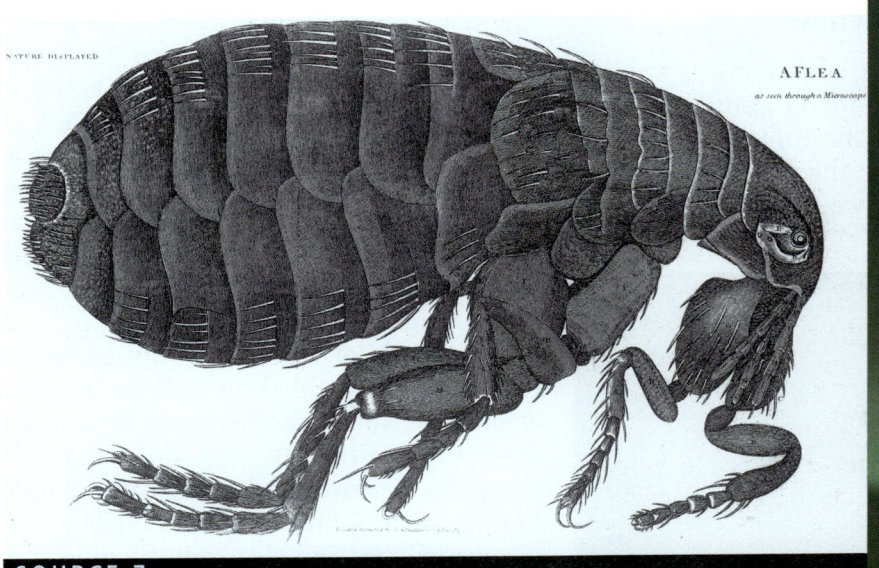

Right: Microscope from the reign of Charles II. With a similar microscope, Robert Hooke was able to make this drawing of a flea.

SOURCE 8

In his poem *Annus Mirabilis* (Latin for Year of Miracles) Dryden describes the Fire of London. In this extract the King arrives on the scene. A year after writing the poem, Dryden was appointed Poet Laureate – the official poet of the royal court.

Now day appears, and with the day the King,
Whose early care had robbed him of his rest:
Far off the cracks of falling houses ring,
And shrieks of subjects pierce his tender breast …

The father of the people open'd wide
His stores, and all the poor with plenty fed;
Thus God's anointed God's own place supplied,
And filled the empty with his daily bread.

SOURCE 9

John Milton (1608–74) painted at the age of 21. He came from a Puritan family in London. When he finished his greatest work, *Paradise Lost*, in 1663, he sold it to a publisher for £10.

the execution of Charles I. He could not understand why God had let the King return.

Paradise Lost tells the Biblical story of Adam and Eve in the Garden of Eden. It is a story of good versus evil, and it is clear that Milton had in mind the good Roundheads and bad Royalists! Not surprisingly, the Royalists hated Milton and at the Restoration he was imprisoned for a short time and banned from official jobs for life. By this time he was blind but he finished his great poem, dictating it to his daughters.

Arts and sciences in the seventeenth century

SOURCE 10

This telescope is probably the one Galileo showed to the Doge, the ruler of Venice, in 1609.

The Starry Messenger

From earliest times, astronomers studied the skies and wondered about the sun, planets and stars. One thing that puzzled them was whether the sun and planets move around us, or we move around them.

The telescope, invented in 1609, helped to provide the answer. Telescopes were first made in Holland. When one was taken to Italy, the government of Venice asked Galileo Galilei, a mathematician, to look at it. He did not think much of the Dutch telescope and designed a far better instrument which showed a clearer image and could magnify nine times. Later, he made one which magnified thirty times.

The people of Venice were interested in telescopes to help their sailors. Galileo wanted to explore the heavens. He was the first to see the hills and valleys of the moon. He discovered that the band of light known as the Milky Way is actually a vast cluster of stars. He also saw the moons of the planet Jupiter and found out more about Venus, another planet. Galileo's discoveries were published in a book he called *The Starry Messenger*.

Galileo soon came to the conclusion that it was the earth, not the sun, which was moving. It was not a new idea. Some ancient Greeks had thought this, and about a hundred years before Galileo a Polish astronomer named Copernicus made a similar suggestion. Nevertheless, it was a dangerous thing to say because the Church taught that the earth was the fixed centre of the Universe and that the planets and stars moved round it. Galileo was cautious and waited many years before putting his ideas in a book.

Galileo's book was an imaginary conversation between two men; one believes the earth is moving and the other believes it is standing still. However Galileo made the character who thought the earth was standing still sound foolish! The Pope guessed which side Galileo was on and put him on trial before a Church court. The astronomer was threatened with torture if he did not change his mind. So he wrote a confession, saying that he no longer believed in 'the false opinion that the sun is the centre of the world and immovable' (**Source 11**). In 1642, the year Galileo died, a man was born who proved his theory had been right. His name was Isaac Newton.

SOURCE 11

Not every Catholic was sure Galileo was wrong about the movement of the earth. This was written by Cardinal Robert Bellarmine, who knew Galileo.

I say that if real proof be found that the sun is fixed and does not revolve around the earth, but the earth around the sun, then it will be necessary, very carefully, to proceed to the explanation of the passages of the Scripture (Bible) which appear to the contrary, and we should rather say that we have misunderstood these (the Scriptures) than to pronounce that to be false which is demonstrated (shown to be true).

74 Ideas and discoveries

Newton and gravity

In August 1665, Cambridge University sent its students home to avoid the plague. One of them was Isaac Newton. At home, he began to fill his time asking questions about the sun, moon and planets. Why did the moon always move round the earth in twenty-seven days? What power kept it travelling at the same speed and in the same orbit? An earlier scientist, William Gilbert, had suggested that the earth might be a giant magnet, pulling objects towards it. But if this were true, why did the moon not crash into the earth?

Newton worked out the speed of the moon, using the known distance between the earth and sun. His calculations proved that the earth, moon and planets were held in place by two forces. One was their own speed. The other was the attraction of the sun's mass, or in other words the pull of gravity. Newton devised a mathematical rule, known as the inverse square law, to measure the strength of this force.

The plague died out and the University opened again. Newton went back to his studies. Before long he became a professor of mathematics and a member of the Royal Society. In 1684 he was asked about the orbit of certain planets. Newton replied that he had already worked them out long ago, in the 'plague year'. He would look up his old notes. But he could not find them so he wrote his calculations out again and included them in a book called *Principia Mathematica* (Mathematical Principles). Published by the Royal Society in 1687, it is one of the most important scientific books ever written (**Source 13**).

The book explains how the universe works to precise mathematical laws. To Newton, God was not a magician, waving a wand to change things unexpectedly, as many people then believed. He was 'the divine clockmaker' whose mechanism, the universe, always moved in exactly the same way. Newton had taught future scientists two important rules. First, they must always test and prove their theories. Second, they should not be puzzled by the disorder of things on the surface but look to see if there is a pattern underneath. In chemistry, such a pattern was found in the nineteenth century when it was discovered that all matter is made up of atoms.

SOURCE 12

Sir Isaac Newton in later life, when he was in charge of the Royal Mint. This painting is by Sir Godfrey Kneller, who also painted the portraits of nine monarchs.

SOURCE 13

In this extract from his *Principia Mathematica*, Newton explains his theory of gravitation.

If it appears ... by experiments and astronomical observations, that all bodies about the earth gravitate towards the earth ... in proportion to the quantity of matter which they contain ... [and] that, on the other hand, our sea gravitates towards the moon; and all the planets towards another; and the comets in like manner towards the sun; we must ... [accept] a principle of mutual (two-way) gravitation.

Arts and sciences in the seventeenth century

Medicine and magic

When the plague struck London in 1665 doctors were helpless. They did not know what caused it so they could not find a cure. In fact, doctors had been misled for centuries by wrong theories about the human body. Since ancient times it had been believed that the body was made up of four 'humours' – blood, yellow bile, black bile and phlegm. Too much of one humour changed a person's character and caused illness. For example, too much blood made people sanguine (high-spirited), whilst yellow bile made them choleric (bad-tempered). A doctor's job was to restore the balance, where necessary, by treatment. The most common remedy was to bleed a patient who was sanguine.

Such false ideas made curing people a hit or miss affair. A doctor might use herbs which did some good, or he might instruct the invalid to wear a charm around the neck or drink water from a skull! Lots of ingredients went into most medicines. A favourite was Oil of Swallow. This was made from herbs, cloves, wax, butter, the foot of an ox and twenty live swallows pounded into a paste. Some medicines were disgusting, such as drinking urine. Others were silly, like putting ointment on a knife that caused a wound, not the wound itself.

Greater knowledge about the body came from dissection – cutting up corpses and examining them. In medieval times this was forbidden by the Church. But during the seventeenth century it became quite common, even though many clergymen disapproved of it (**Source 15**). Interest in dissection increased with the invention of the microscope. This became as useful in the study of biology and medicine as the telescope was in astronomy.

> **SOURCE 14**
>
> Drawing from a seventeenth-century medical textbook by John Banister of Glasgow. A pig is being dissected while a monkey awaits its turn.

> **SOURCE 15**
>
> Celia Fiennes was a keen traveller who wrote an account of her journeys around Britain in the late seventeenth century. Here she describes a dissection in Newcastle.
>
> I went to see the Barber Surgeons Hall … there I saw a room with a round table in it, railed round with seats or benches for the conveniency in their dissecting … and reading lectures on all parts; there was two bodies that had been anatomised (dissected), one the bones were fastened with wires, the other had had the flesh boiled off [but] some of the ligaments remained and dried with it, and so the parts were held together by its own muscles.

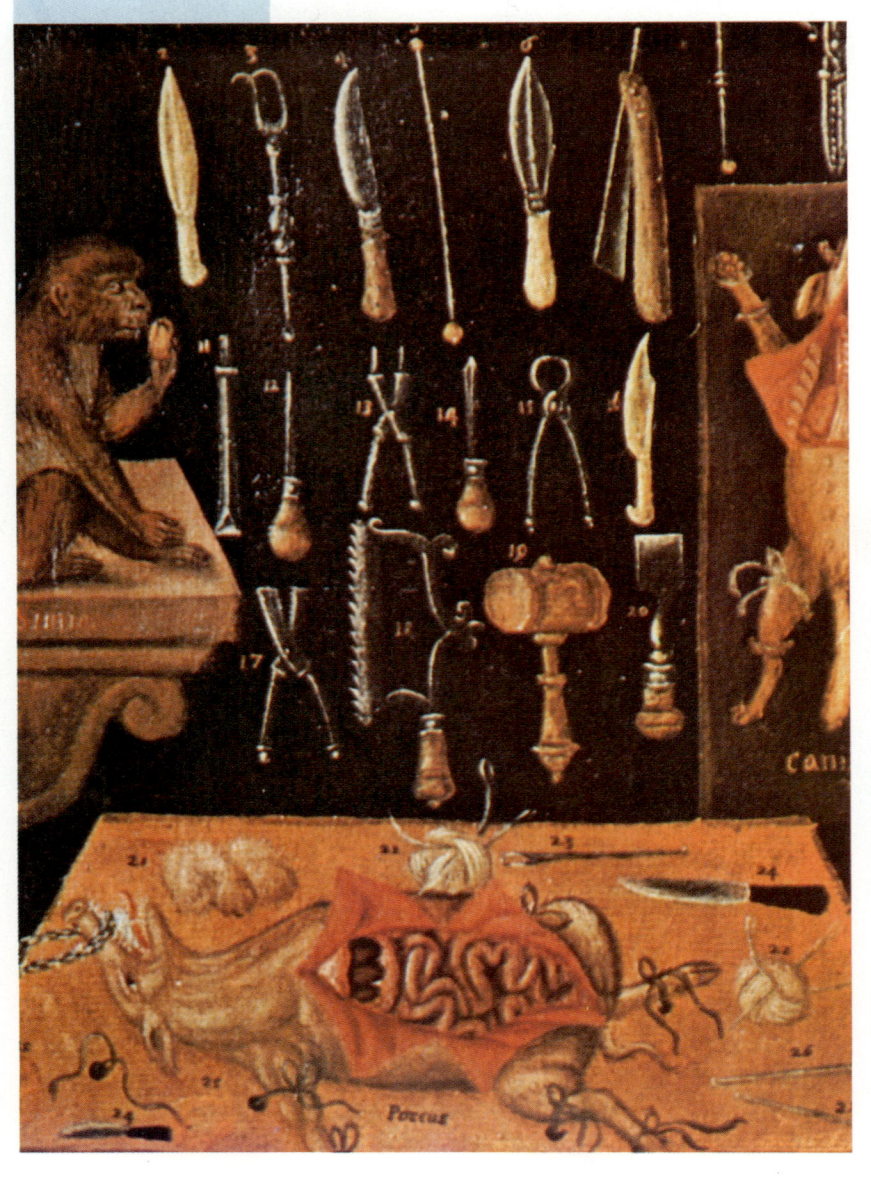

Ideas and discoveries

SOURCE 16

This is a model of the anatomy theatre at Padua University, where William Harvey (1578–1657) trained to be a doctor. It was designed so that students could watch a dissection from the circular galleries.

The circulation of the blood

The most important medical discovery of the seventeenth century came about because of dissection. It was made by William Harvey who trained as a doctor at Padua University in Italy (**Source 16**). Later he worked at a London hospital and was physician (doctor) to King Charles I. Harvey's studies made him wonder how blood moved inside the body. At that time it was believed that the heart pumped blood out and then sucked it back again, rather like the tidal movement of the sea. But Harvey suspected that blood moved one way only, circulating round the body.

QUESTIONS

1 What was the idea behind a doctor asking his patient to wear a charm?

2 Why do you think churchmen disapproved of dissecting human bodies?

3 Can you think of any reason why it was an executed criminal's body that Harvey got for his experiment?

4 How is Source 17 relevant to Harvey's theory about the circulation of the blood?

Arts and sciences in the seventeenth century

This theory left an important question unanswered. If the movement of blood was in one direction only, how did it get from the right *ventricle* (chamber) of the heart to the left ventricle because there was no way through the heart? Harvey showed that it went from one chamber to the other through the lungs. He did this by carrying out a grim experiment on the body of a criminal who had been hanged. When he tied up the passages from the right side of the heart to the lungs and filled the right ventricle with water, nothing came through to the left ventricle. But when he loosened these arteries and veins, blood and water poured through. Harvey had discovered the circulation of the blood – and paved the way for others to show how blood carries oxygen from the lungs round the body.

Harvey's theory was thought crazy at first. He was so afraid of being laughed at that he had his book, *On the Motion of the Heart and Blood*, published in Germany, in 1628. Later, people changed their minds as more tests proved the truth of what he had written (**Source 18**). At the end of Harvey's life, as he lay dying, doctors made him worse by bleeding. It was a sad end for a man who, in his Will, instructed the Royal College of Physicians 'to search out and study the secrets of nature by experiment'.

SOURCE 17

This drawing comes from William Harvey's book, *On the Motion of the Heart and Blood* (1628). Because the arm at the top is bandaged, the vein swells and small valves (labelled with letters) show up. In the lower drawing, the finger pressed on the vein stops the flow of blood. But the vein does not refill between H and O because the valve at O is one-way and only allows the blood to move towards the heart.

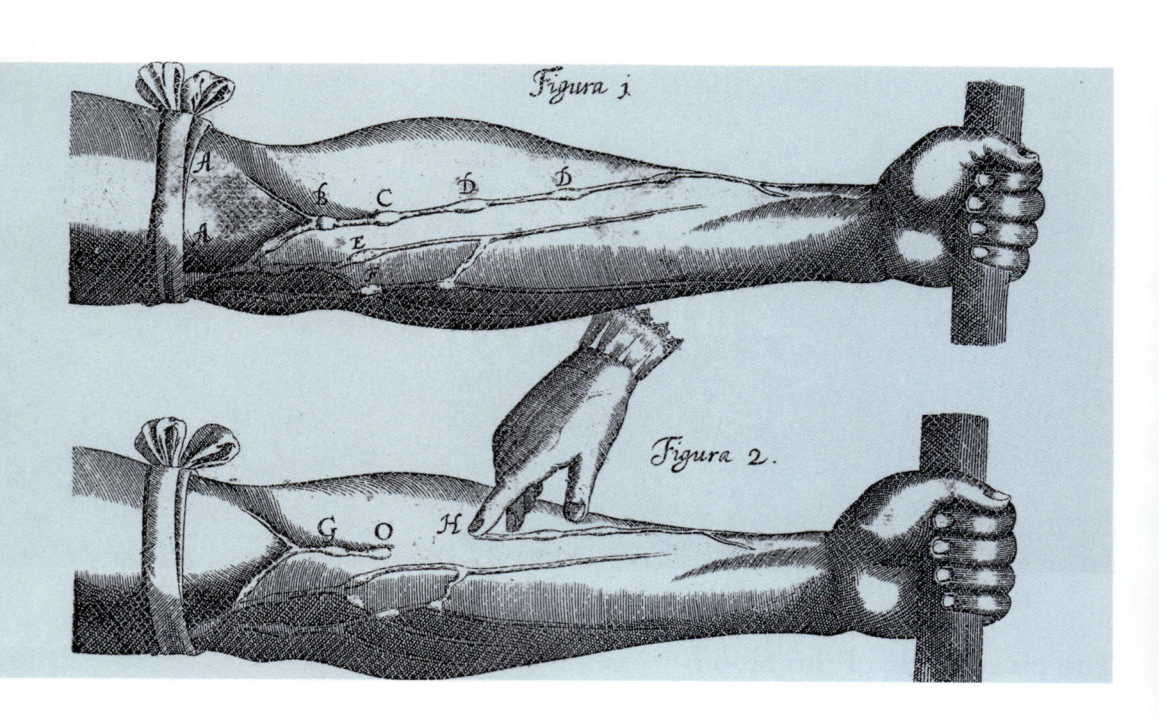

SOURCE 18

John Aubrey (1626–1697) wrote about many of the famous men of his time. This comes from his biography of William Harvey.

I have heard him (Harvey) say, that after his book of the Circulation of the Blood came out, that he fell mightily in his Practice (lost many patients), and that 'twas believed by the vulgar that he was crack-brained; and all the Physicians (doctors) were against his Opinion … In about 20 or 30 years time, it was received in all the Universities of the world … He is the only man, perhaps, that ever lived to see his own theories believed during his life-time.

Ideas and discoveries

Assessment tasks

A Knowledge and understanding

1 Describe the similarities and differences between St Paul's and any other cathedral you have seen in Britain. (Look carefully at the picture on page 71, and try to find more pictures – or, better still, visit St Paul's if you can.)

2 Give as many examples as you can from this period to show how one scientific invention or discovery often depended on another.

3 Explain how the advance of science in the seventeenth century clashed with:
a superstition and belief in magic;
b the teachings of the Catholic Church.

B Interpretations and sources

4 Here are three modern historians' views of the Royal Society.

> (i) Shortly after the Restoration, the Royal Society was founded ... At their weekly meetings ... the experiments ranged [over] all nature ... In their boundless curiosity, [members] were laying the foundations of the modern world.
> (A. Bryant, 1931)

> (ii) Though ... the Society was the lively centre of talk and inquiry, it tried too hard over too broad a field that ranged from tin-mining to English grammar and from statistics to bee-keeping. The great discoveries of the ... Stuart age were ... achieved by individuals, moved by the restless spirit of the times.
> (M. Ashley, 1964)

> (iii) The Royal Society experienced ... difficulties in distinguishing genuinely important matters from the vast mass of trivia (unimportant things) ... Historians have often grossly overestimated the Society's importance.
> (R. Briggs, 1969)

a What are the points of disagreement between these accounts?
b Which do you think is nearest the truth, and why (re-read Source 6 before you answer)?
c Which account do you think is nearest to the seventeenth-century view of the Royal Society, and why?

5 Compare Sources 1 and 8. Which source do you think is the most useful in helping us to understand Charles II? Give reasons for your answer.

6 What can be learnt from the sources in this chapter (particularly Sources 6, 11, 14, 15, 16, 17 and 19) about:
a seventeenth-century attitudes towards science;
b the sorts of difficulties scientists at that time had to overcome?

8 'The Glorious Revolution'

James II overthrown

In November 1688 King James II of England ordered a weathervane to be fixed to the roof of the Banqueting Hall in London. He was expecting an invasion from Holland and, in the days of sailing ships, he needed to know which way the wind was blowing. An easterly wind would drive the Dutch fleet towards the English coast and make it difficult for English warships to sail out of the Thames. James said the weathervane would show him whether the wind was Catholic or Protestant! This was because he was a Catholic and his enemies were Dutch Protestants led by their prince, William of Orange. It was also a family quarrel because William was married to James's eldest daughter, Mary.

For days the wind blew from the east. The Dutch ships, loaded with men, horses and supplies, sailed down the Channel and anchored at Torbay in Devon. William was able to land his army safely and begin his march towards London. In the exciting days which followed, Protestant clergymen thanked God for the 'Protestant Wind'.

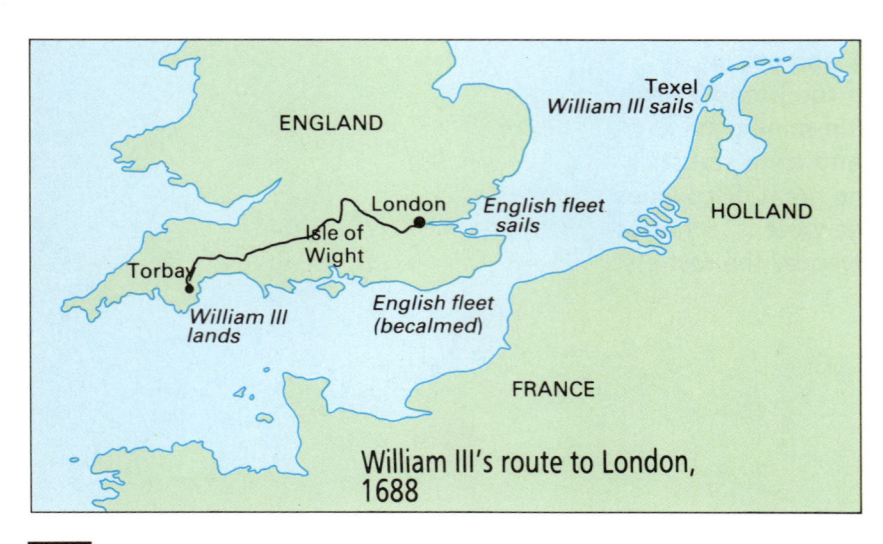

William III's route to London, 1688

Tories and Whigs

The story of William's invasion in 1688 begins some years earlier. Charles II, who reigned before James, had no legitimate children but several by other women, including a son, the Duke of Monmouth. Under English law this meant that, should he die first, Charles would be followed by his brother, the Catholic James. This alarmed Protestants. Catholics were still strongly disliked in England, where there had been laws against them since the time of Elizabeth I (see Chapter 3). They were not allowed to be MPs, army officers, justices of the peace or government officials. They were even barred from going to university. To many Protestants, having a Catholic king was unthinkable.

During Charles II's reign a group of MPs and Lords had tried to stop James succeeding to the throne. These men, known as Whigs, put a Bill before Parliament suggesting that either Mary or the Duke of Monmouth should reign if Charles died first. Many other MPs and Lords were against this suggestion. They were called Tories. There were angry debates in Parliament and riots as supporters of the Bill tried to whip up fear of Catholic rule (**Source 2**). In the end the Bill was defeated, and its chief supporters, including Monmouth, fled abroad to escape their enemies. Whig and Tory later became the names of the first English political parties.

Charles died suddenly in 1685 and James became King. Within months, there were two attempts to overthrow

SOURCE 1

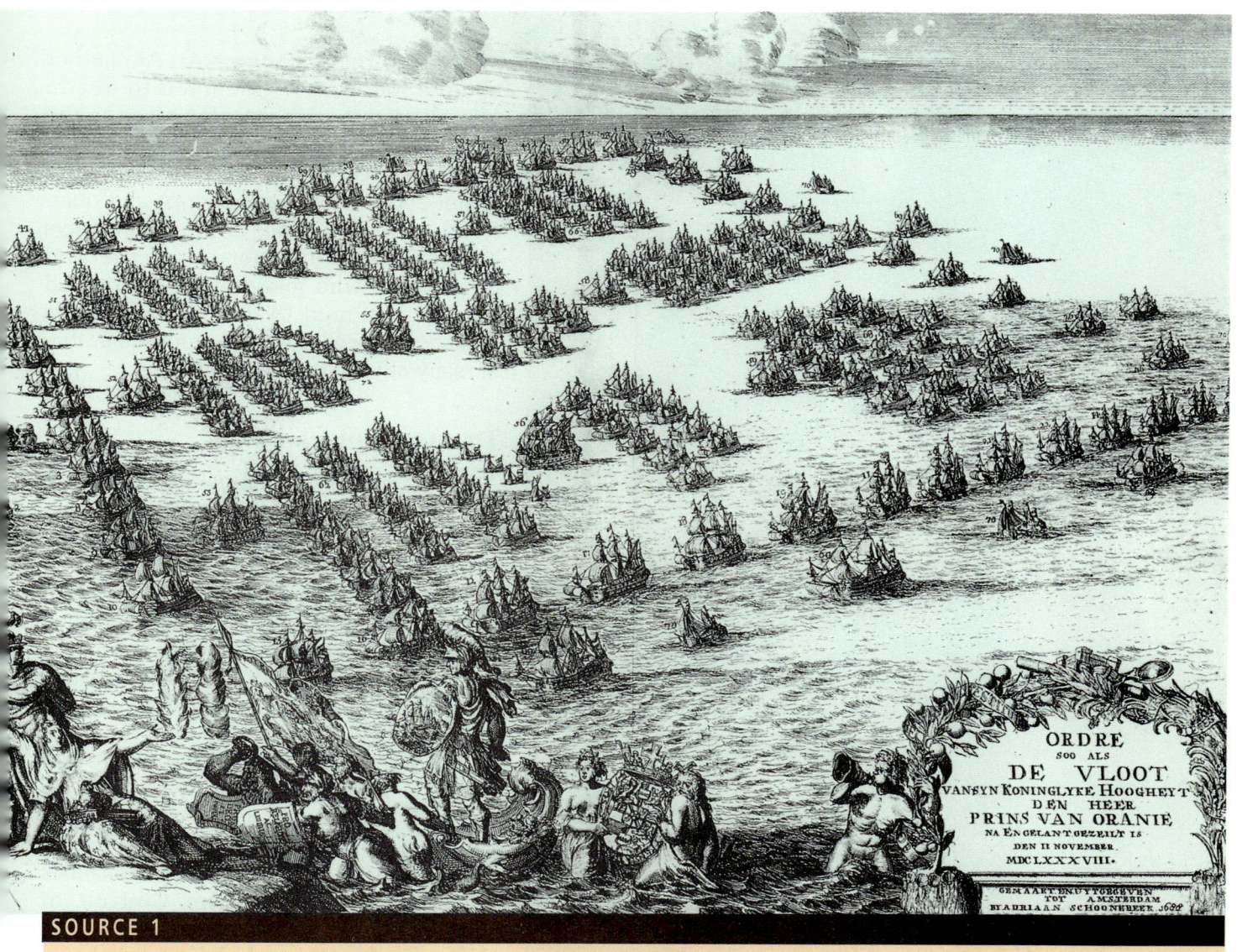

This Dutch engraving shows William of Orange's invasion fleet at sea, November 1688. It was risky to attempt such a large-scale operation so late in the year. The Dutch fleet could easily have been damaged or destroyed by autumn gales.

him. In May, a rebellion by Protestants in Scotland was crushed. In June, Monmouth landed in Dorset and proclaimed himself King. He was handsome, popular and a Protestant, so he hoped to topple James. But few important men joined him, and in July his small army was defeated by royal troops at Sedgemoor in Somerset. Monmouth tried to reach the coast to escape, but he was captured near Ringwood in Hampshire, taken to London and executed.

James sent the Lord Chief Justice, George Jeffreys, to the West Country to

SOURCE 2

This comes from a pamphlet published in 1679 by Protestants aiming to arouse fear of Catholic rule. Smithfield, in London, is where many Protestants were burned in the reign of the Catholic Queen, Mary Tudor (1553–8).

First, imagine you see a whole town (London) in flame, caused this second time by the same Popish malice (Catholic spite) which set it on fire before (in 1666) … You behold troops of Papists (Catholics) ravishing (raping) your wives and daughters, dashing your little children's brains out against walls, plundering your houses and cutting your throats … Casting your eyes towards Smithfield … you see your father or mother tied to a stake in the midst of the flames.

James II overthrown

punish the rebels (**Source 4**). Altogether about 1300 were condemned to death. Three-quarters of these were given to the Queen and courtiers to be sold as labourers in the West Indies and North America. About 200 were hanged, drawn and quartered – the usual fate of rebels. Jeffreys has gone down in history as a cruel and unjust man who joked as he sentenced men and women to death. In fact, his behaviour in court was no worse than that of many other judges of the time.

The warming-pan baby

After the defeat of Monmouth's rebellion, James seemed safe on the throne. Many Protestants, however, were suspicious and worried. James had Catholic advisers and he allowed Catholics to worship openly in London. Was he about to turn the country Catholic? He certainly seemed determined to make life easier for Catholics because he soon began to ignore the laws against them. For instance, he appointed Catholics as officers in the army and tried to get them elected as MPs. Finally, in 1687, he temporarily cancelled all the laws against Catholics by what was known as a Declaration of Indulgence. Nonconformists (Protestants outside the Church of England) were also freed from such laws.

The Declaration of Indulgence led to a crisis. The Church of England saw its grip on national life threatened. Seven bishops refused to have it read out in their churches, saying it was illegal. They were arrested and put on trial by order of the King. As fears of a Catholic takeover grew, Mary Beatrice, James's second wife, gave birth to a son (10 June 1688). Males always succeed to the throne before females under English law. So the new prince, brought up as a Catholic, would get the Crown when James died – not Mary, or her younger sister, Anne.

Protestants refused to believe the bad news (**Source 6**). They said the baby was not Mary Beatrice's child but a tradesman's son, smuggled into the Queen's bedroom in a warming-pan (a long-handled

SOURCE 3

King James II, painted by Sir Godfrey Kneller. James had been brought up as a Protestant but turned Catholic in 1672. His first wife, who died in 1671, was a Protestant, and so were the two daughters of this marriage, Anne and Mary.

SOURCE 4

John Tutchin took part in Monmouth's rebellion but escaped with his life. Here he gives his opinion of Judge Jeffreys.

His treatment of the rebels is not to be equalled in history ... People could not offend so much as to deserve the punishment he inflicted. A certain joy and pleasure grinned from his brutal soul through his bloody eyes, whenever he was sentencing any of the poor souls to death and torment.

pan with a lid, filled with live coals to warm bedclothes). This was just a rumour. The baby was James's son, but, as a spy reported to William, 'Be it true or false, the people will never believe it'.

The fall of James II

Soon after the birth of James's son, the seven bishops were found not guilty; the jury decided that the King had no right to issue the Declaration of Indulgence (**Source 8**). A secret letter, signed in code by three Tories, three Whigs and a bishop, was smuggled to Holland by an admiral disguised as an ordinary sailor. It invited

SOURCE 5

This Dutch print shows James II's Queen, Mary Beatrice, rocking the cradle of her infant son. The priest embracing the Queen is Father Edward Petrie, a member of the royal household. It was rumoured in some quarters that Petrie was the father of the child.

SOURCE 6

Anne, stepsister of James's newborn child, was not present when the boy was born. She wrote this to her sister, Mary, in Holland.

You can't imagine the concern and vexation (irritation) I have been in, that I should be so unfortunate as to be out of town (London) when the Queen was brought to bed (to give birth), for I shall never know whether the child be true or false. It may be it is our brother, but God only knows, for she (the Queen) never took care to … give people any demonstration of it (her pregnancy) … 'tis possible it may be her child, but where one believes, a thousand do not.

SOURCE 7

The seven bishops leave the Tower of London to go to their trial, June 1688.

SOURCE 8

John Evelyn was a lawyer who served under James II. These comments on the trial of the seven bishops come from his diary, which was discovered in a laundry basket in 1817.

29 June 1688 They (the bishops) appeared … the jury were eleven for an acquittal (not guilty); but one, Arnold a brewer, would not consent. At length he agreed with the others … When this was heard there was great rejoicing; and there was a lane (two lines) of people from the King's Bench (court) to the waterside, on their knees, as the Bishops passed … to beg their blessing. Bonfires were made that night, and bells rung, which was taken very ill (badly) at Court.

William to come to England to 'save' the kingdom from a Catholic plot (**Source 9**).

William was willing to come for reasons of his own. For years he had been at war with the French Catholic King, Louis XIV, whose armies had invaded Holland. What if a Catholic England joined forces with France? Louis and James were already far too friendly in William's opinion. It would be better all round if his own wife, Mary, became Queen of England in place of her father.

At first, James tried to put up a fight. He took command of the royal army at Salisbury but found that his men were deserting to William. Even his younger daughter, Anne, changed sides and went to meet her brother-in-law. William was able to march his troops to London without firing a shot. James sent his wife and baby to France where Louis promised to look after them. When he tried to follow, some fishermen mistook him for a Catholic priest and sent him back to London under guard.

This did not suit William. He had decided it would be best if he became king himself, and this would be easier if James was out of the way. So James was allowed to escape from the palace through an unguarded door. He sailed to France just before Christmas 1688. When the news got out, Protestant mobs ran riot in London, destroying Catholic chapels.

The 1689 Settlement

In February 1689, Parliament invited William and Mary to reign as joint monarchs. This marked the start of a new kind of monarchy. As king, William could appoint his ministers, deal with foreign governments and run the country from day to day. But there were important differences from the way things had been done in the past.

William was king because Parliament had chosen him, not because of any Divine Right. He was bound by strict rules set out in a Bill of Rights and other laws. In future, Parliament alone could raise taxes, make laws and control the army. No monarch could change this, or alter laws once they were made. Parliament was to meet at least every three years, and could not sit longer than three years without a fresh election (**Source 10**).

SOURCE 9

Here is part of the letter of invitation to William of Orange, sent on the night the seven bishops were found not guilty.

We have great satisfaction to find your Highness is so ready and willing to give us such assistance ... The People are generally so dissatisfied with the conduct of the Government in relation to their religion ... that your Highness may be assured there are nineteen parts of twenty ... desirous of a change ... Some of the gentry and nobility will venture themselves (risk their lives) with your Highness at your first landing.

QUESTIONS

1. The story of 'the warming-pan baby' was false. But what reason might the King and Queen have had for carrying out such a hoax?

2. Can you think of a reason why Anne (Source 6) might have preferred not to know the truth about Mary Beatrice's baby?

3. Why do you think the invitation to William of Orange was signed by an equal number of Tories and Whigs?

4. Can you think of a reason why the letter to William was written in code and why the admiral who carried it disguised himself as an ordinary sailor?

SOURCE 10

Here are some of the most important statements in the Bill of Rights, 1689.

That the pretended power of suspending (temporarily cancelling) laws ... without consent of Parliament is illegal ...

That the levying of money for ... the use of the Crown ... without the consent of Parliament is illegal ...

That the raising or keeping of a standing (permanent) army ... in time of peace, unless it be with consent of Parliament, is against law.

The key to Parliament's power over the Crown lay in its control of money. William needed far more money than any previous king of England. This was because his own country, Holland, was at war with France, and England soon joined in when Louis XIV supported James's right to the throne. Only Parliament, through taxes, could finance the long wars which followed. Never again would an English monarch be able to run the country from royal income alone. William began by borrowing £1,200,000 for his wars. He agreed to pay 8½ per cent interest annually and allowed the goldsmiths who loaned the money to form the Bank of England. This sum became the National Debt, a permanent part of government finances.

Under the Bill of Rights, no Catholic could be king or queen. No member of the royal family could even marry a Catholic without losing their rights to the throne. The succession to the throne was settled by Parliament. William and Mary would be followed by their children. If they had no children, the Crown would pass to Anne. Mary died childless in 1694. Anne gave birth to seventeen children but they all died. When the last child, a boy, died in 1701, the Protestant descendants of James I's daughter, Elizabeth, became heirs to the throne after Anne.

The Whigs liked this Settlement so much that they called the events of 1688–9 'The Glorious Revolution'. The Tories would have preferred James to remain, with reduced powers. Since he had left the country this was impossible. In several ways the revolution *was* glorious. It brought new freedoms. In 1694 Nonconformists, but not Catholics, were allowed to worship freely, although they were still barred from official jobs and the universities. And in 1695 the government dropped the law which required all publications to be licenced – and therefore censored. This led to a flood of newsheets and magazines. In 1702 *The Daily Courant*, the world's first daily newspaper, was published.

SOURCE 11

The first Bank of England building in Graces Hall, London. The Bank issued paper money, including bills of exchange (written orders to pay a certain sum on a stated day) and promissory notes (written promises to pay). With money of this kind available, trading deals could be arranged without transporting large amounts of coinage.

SOURCE 12

Front page of *The Daily Courant*, the world's first daily newspaper, published in London in 1702. How does it compare with the front page of a newspaper today?

James II overthrown **85**

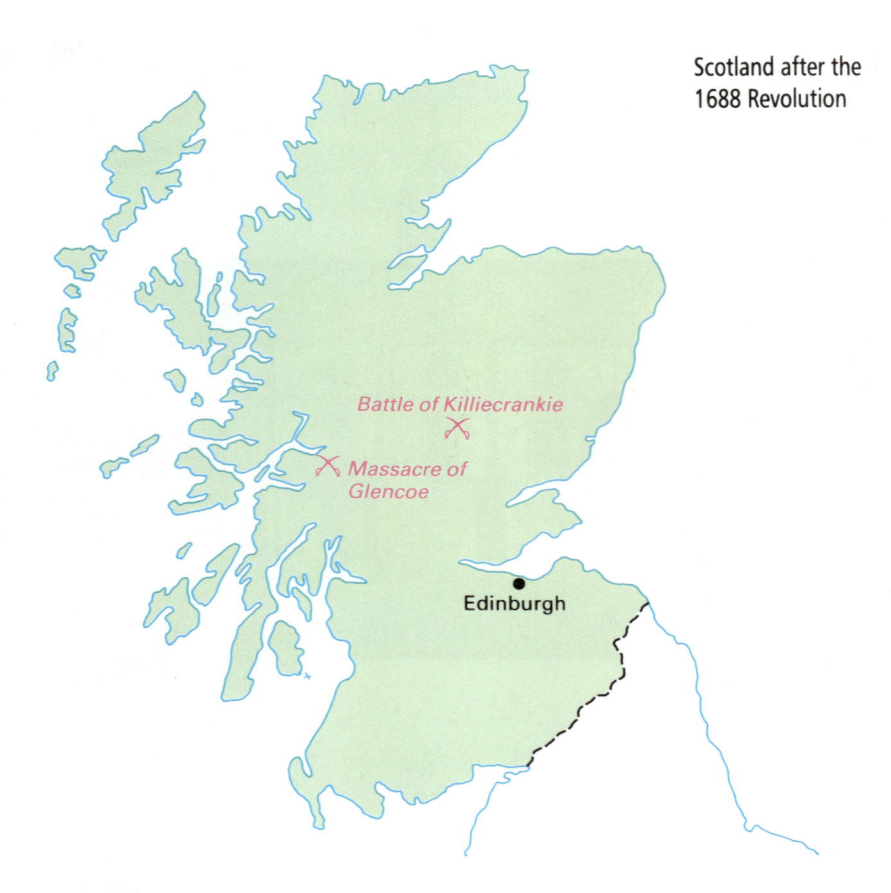

Scotland after the 1688 Revolution

Scotland – the massacre at Glencoe

Scotland took no part in the 'Glorious Revolution'. Opinions about it were divided. Protestant Scots in the lowland areas were pleased at the changes, but most of those living in the Highlands were not. Here, the people belonged to large groups called clans. These clans were ruled by chiefs who were old-fashioned in their ways and, in some cases, Catholics.

Highlanders scratched a bare living from the land and often fought bitter feuds with each other (**Source 13**). When news of the revolution reached them they rose in revolt. Their leader, Viscount Dundee, won a battle against Scots loyal to William at Killiecrankie (July 1689) but he was killed in the moment of victory. His men marched on to Dunkeld but their attacks were driven off by Protestants. Disheartened, the clansmen drifted home and the rebellion collapsed.

At first the English government was merciful. William offered to pardon all rebel chiefs who took an oath of loyalty to him by 1 January 1692. However, the chief of the MacDonalds was delayed by bad weather and took the oath six days late. William was advised by his minister for Scotland, Sir John Dalrymple, to make an example of the troublesome chief and his clan.

Captain Campbell of Glenlyon was sent to Glencoe, where the MacDonalds lived, with 100 soldiers. His instructions were to kill 'the old fox and his sons'. The MacDonalds and Campbells had long been enemies so the MacDonalds were suspicious. Nevertheless there was little they could do except treat the Campbells as guests. After dark on 13 February the Campbell troops attacked without warning (**Source 14**). The chief and thirty-six of his clan, including four women and a child, were killed. Survivors fled across the mountains under cover of a snowstorm. William was blamed for the massacre of Glencoe and his rule was hated in the Highlands.

SOURCE 13

Here an Englishman, Edward Burt, tells of the obedience of Highlanders to their chief. He visited Scotland in the early years of the eighteenth century.

The ordinary Highlanders esteem (think) it a virtue to love their chief and pay him a blind obedience although it is against the government, the laws of the Kingdom and even the laws of God. He is their idol and they profess (claim) to know no other king … I happened to be at the house of a certain chief when another chief told him that some of his clan had not behaved well to me … He clapped his hand to his broadsword and said, if I required it, he would send me two or three of their heads.

SOURCE 14

This letter was sent to Captain Campbell of Glenlyon by Major Robert Duncasson, acting on government orders. It is dated the day before the massacre of Glencoe.

Sir,
You are hereby ordered to fall upon the rebels, the MacDonalds of Glencoe, and to put to the sword all under seventy. You are to take special care that the old fox (the chief) and his sons do not escape. This you are to do at five of the clock precisely … By that time … I'll strive to be with you with a stronger party [of soldiers] … This is the King's special command for the good and safety of the country.

'The Glorious Revolution'

SOURCE 15

The pass of Glencoe, home of the MacDonalds and scene of the massacre of 1692.

'King Billy' in Ireland

In Ireland, Catholics enjoyed freedom of worship under James II. They were also allowed their own parliament. They knew what the 1688 Revolution would mean for them so they, too, rose in revolt. In 1689 James landed in Ireland to help them, assisted by French troops. Only two towns, Londonderry and Enniskellen, held out for the government, defended by Protestant Irish. The siege of Londonderry lasted 105 days. The townsfolk were so short of food that they ate dogs and rats and drank horses' blood. Finally, an English warship managed to get into the harbour with supplies. The Catholic army gave up and marched away.

England was now at war with France. A French army was in Ireland. William feared that if the country fell into the hands of James and his French allies it might be used as a base for an invasion of England. So in June 1690 William landed in the north of Ireland with an army. James decided to fight him beside the river

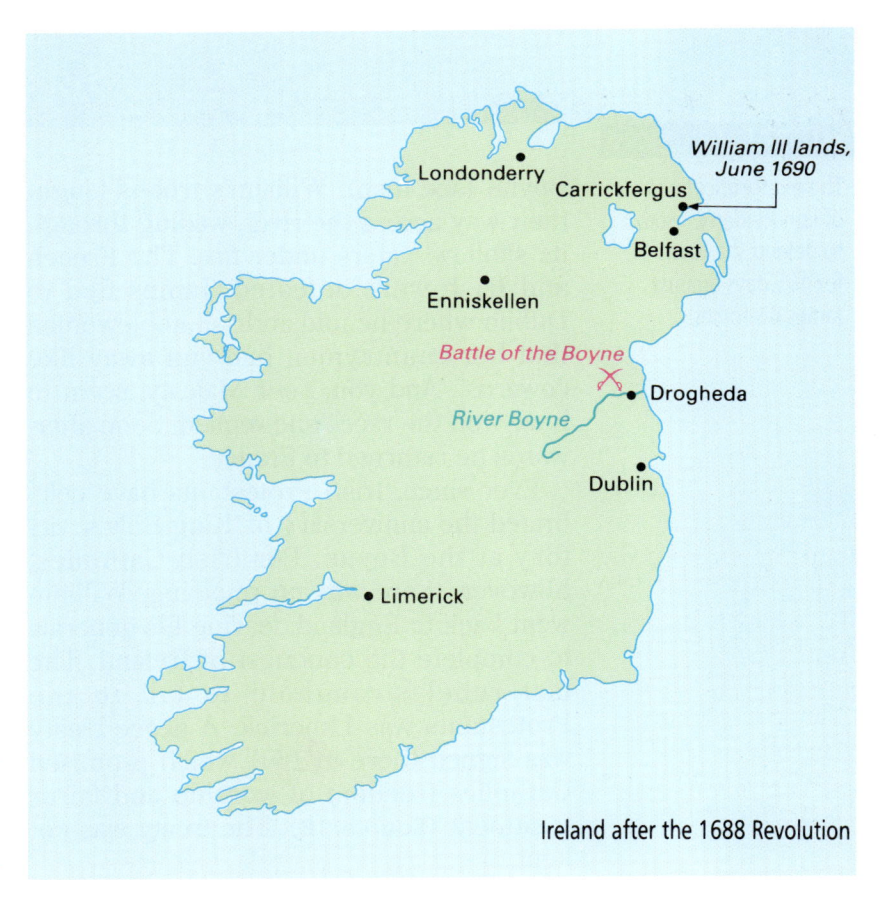

Ireland after the 1688 Revolution

SOURCE 16

The old fortifications of Londonderry, used to defend the town for 105 days against James II's forces.

Boyne (see map). William's troops fought their way across the river, wading through its shallow waters under fire. The French and Irish were defeated. James fled to Dublin where he told an Irish noblewoman that her countrymen had run away like cowards. 'And you, your Majesty, seem to have won the race', she replied. Soon afterwards he returned to France.

Ever since, Irish Protestants have celebrated the anniversary of 'King Billy's' victory at the Boyne. For Irish Catholics, however, there was no rejoicing. William went back to England, leaving his generals to complete the conquest of Ireland. The last rebel stronghold to fall to the Protestants was Limerick. A peace treaty was signed there in 1691 which promised Catholics freedom of worship and fairer treatment (**Source 18**). The treaty was not kept.

During the eighteenth century, Catholics continued to be barred from official jobs and from being MPs, lawyers and army officers. In some cases they were even stopped from being schoolteachers and craftsmen. In England, such restrictions affected only a small part of the population. But in Ireland they affected the great majority. The results of such unfairness are still with us today.

QUESTIONS

1. What was the point of getting the Campbells to stay with the MacDonalds, rather than sending an army to Glencoe straight away?
2. What were Irish Catholics afraid would happen once James was no longer king?
3. Why were the French willing to support James II's Irish campaign in 1689?
4. Why might William be surprised to know that he is a hero in Northern Ireland?

'The Glorious Revolution'

SOURCE 17

William III on horseback, shown at the battle of the Boyne. Although a brave soldier, he was not as dashing as this painting suggests.

SOURCE 18

This is the First Article (section) of the Treaty of Limerick (1691) with its 'broken promise'.

That the Roman Catholics of this kingdom shall enjoy such privileges in the exercise of their religion as … they did enjoy in the reign of Charles II; and their majesties (William and Mary), as soon as their affairs will permit them to summon a parliament in this kingdom, will endeavour to give the Roman Catholics such further security … as may preserve them from disturbance on account of their religion.

James II overthrown

Assessment tasks

A Knowledge and understanding

1 Here are some possible short term, or immediate, causes of the 1688 Revolution.

- The trial of the seven bishops.
- King James had Catholic advisers in this government.
- The Declaration of Indulgence, 1687.
- James allowed Catholics to worship openly.
- The birth of James's son in 1688.

a Put these causes in what you consider to be their order of importance. Give reasons for your answer.

b The causes of the Revolution go back much further than James II's brief reign. Make a list of *long term* causes, in order of importance, giving reasons in each case.

2 The writer of the following, Henry Pitman, took part in the Duke of Monmouth's rebellion. He was sentenced to be transported to the West Indies, but pardoned in 1689.

> Certain persons called us (the prisoners) out of our cells and told us … we would get the King's Grace and Favour (pardon) … if we gave an account of where we joined the Duke's army … Otherwise we could expect no mercy. In this way they drew us into a confession of our guilt … So Jeffreys knew beforehand our particular crimes and had received orders from the King … who and what numbers to execute.

Compare this account with Source 4.
a In what ways do they contradict each other?
b Which do you think is nearer the truth, and why?

3 What was the attitude of each of the following to William III becoming king?
a English Tories.
b Scottish Highlanders.
c Irish Catholics.
d English Whigs.
e Irish Protestants.

B Interpretations and sources

4 The Republic of Ireland, which is mainly Catholic, became independent of the United Kingdom in 1922. Six counties in the North, where the majority of the people are Protestant, are still part of the UK. Here are two sources which show the different attitudes in the Republic and Northern Ireland towards 'King Billy'.

(i) In that part of Ireland which achieved independence in 1922 the public monuments to William III were soon destroyed. In 1923 a … party from the Irish army garrison in Drogheda drove out along the Boyne and destroyed the obelisk (monument marking the site of the battle) with a landmine … In 1929 an attempt was made to blow up the statue of William III in Dublin. It proved somewhat ineffective, but the city council declared it should be removed in any case because it was 'a traffic hazard'.
(Rex Cathcart, 1988)

(ii) On the right is a modern wall-painting in Londonderry (known to Catholics as Derry) in Northern Ireland. It shows the siege of the town being relieved and William III at the battle of the Boyne.

a Why would the people of the Republic of Ireland wish to destroy statues of William III? What

'The Glorious Revolution'

authority would have put them up in the first place?

b Why do many people in Northern Ireland want to remember the events shown in the wall-painting? What section of the Northern Ireland population might object to such a painting, and why?

c Can you explain why Irish people in both the Republic and the North are still so interested in a King who died nearly 300 years ago?

5 Look again at Source 5. Why do you think the artist has represented the royal birth in this way? What purpose might the artist have had in making this picture?

6 a What do Sources 2, 6, 8 and 9 tell you about the attitudes of James II's subjects towards his rule?

b Do you think these sources are reliable? Give reasons for your answer in each case.

9 Britain United

Crown, Parliament and Union with Scotland

SOURCE 1

Queen Anne (1702–14) painted in about 1690 by Sir Godfrey Kneller. As she was a Stuart, her right to the Crown was not disputed. And her strong support for the Church of England helped to make her popular.

Although the Stuart kings came originally from Scotland, they rarely visited their homeland after James I rode south in 1603 (see page 49). The Scots had little say in English affairs. Moreover the Scottish war against the Prayer Book in 1639, and the help given to Parliament during the Civil War, ended unhappily. Scotland was conquered by the New Model Army and for a time it was ruled from England.

Scotland – the poor relation

The Scots got back their own Parliament after the 1688 Revolution. But the country remained neglected and poor. It had few industries and its backward farming was often unable to support its small population of about 1 million. People died of starvation whenever the harvest was bad. As well as growing oats and barley, the Scots reared sheep and cattle. But most of their livestock had to be sold over the border to pay for essential imports from England (**Source 2**). Roughly 30,000 animals were driven south each year to English markets.

Scotland was treated as a foreign country by England and not allowed to trade with English colonies overseas. In 1695 the Scots tried to start an empire of their own. They founded a colony at Darien in Central America. The English were against the plan and did nothing to help the settlers when Spain claimed the territory and sent in troops. After five years the colony had to be abandoned. Many lives and all the investors' money had been lost. Clearly, Scotland would find it hard to stand alone as a trading nation.

One answer to Scotland's difficulties would be union with England. This had been suggested several times since 1660 but there was strong opposition to it on both sides of the border. Many Scots wanted to remain independent. The English did not want to share their wealth. One man summed up English feelings when he said that, if union came, 'all the advantage we shall have will be no more than a man gets by marrying a beggar'.

Act of Union, 1707

Attitudes towards union changed very quickly, for two main reasons. First, the Scots, angry over the Darien disaster, hinted that they might choose their own monarch when Queen Anne died. If they did, there would probably be war between the two countries. Second, when another war broke out between England and France in 1702, the Scottish Parliament said they might not join in against France. To the English this was unthinkable. Large numbers of Scotsmen were serving in the army and navy. If they deserted in wartime it could be disastrous. Furthermore, if Scotland stayed neutral, the French would have a 'backdoor' to invade England.

The crisis came in 1703. The Scottish Parliament passed an Act which stated that Scotland must be consulted about going to war, and the Scots alone would decide who their next monarch should be. The English Parliament hit back with two threats. It pointed out that, should the Scots take either of these actions, the cattle trade would be stopped. This would mean ruin and hardship for Scottish merchants and farmers. And the English added that all Scots living in England would be treated as aliens (foreigners).

Despite all the threats, both sides stood to gain from a closer relationship. Union would make England safer in time of war. It would benefit the whole of Scotland and make many Scottish gentlemen wealthy. Even so, few people were enthusiastic about it. The Scots had a proud history as an independent nation. The English looked upon the Scots as their traditional enemies. But circumstances were driving the two countries together. As the English grumbled and the Scots rioted (**Source 4**),

> **SOURCE 2**
>
> Andrew Fletcher, a leading member of the Scottish Parliament, had this to say about relations between England and Scotland before the Union – which he voted against.
>
> Our money was spent in England and not among ourselves; the furniture of our houses and the best of our clothes and equipage was bought in London, and though particular Scots ... had many great and profitable places at court ... yet that was no advantage to our country, which was totally neglected like a farm managed by servants and not under the eye of the master.

> **SOURCE 3**
>
> Glasgow, Scotland's main port on the west coast, in the early eighteenth century.

> **SOURCE 4**
>
> A writer, Daniel Defoe, was sent to Scotland by the government to gain support for the Union. Here he describes what happened when the Duke of Hamilton, who was against it, appeared in the streets in his sedan chair (an enclosed seat carried on poles by servants).
>
> It had been whispered about for several days that the rabble would rise, and come up to the Parliament house, and cry out 'No Union'; that they would carry away the honours (Crown jewels) ... to the castle ... But the first appearance of anything mobbish was, that very day, when the Duke (of Hamilton) ... came down in his chair from the (parliament) house, the mob following him, shouting and crying out 'God bless your grace for standing up against the Union'.

representatives from both countries met to seek an agreement. On 1 May 1707 an Act of Union joined together England, Wales and Scotland. The United Kingdom of Great Britain was born.

Scotland got better terms than might have been expected. England needed a peaceful, friendly and Protestant Scotland on its doorstep and was prepared to give a lot to get it. Under the Act, Scottish merchants enjoyed free trade with England and the English colonies. Scotland also kept its own laws and courts, its schools and universities and its Presbyterian Church. The Scottish Parliament was abolished, but 45 Scots MPs and 16 lords joined the British Parliament. Both countries were to use the same currency and pay the same taxes. However £400,000 compensation was given to Scots who had lost money in the Darien disaster.

Many Scots never agreed with the Union and treated 1 May as a day of mourning! The vote in the Scottish Parliament had been 116 for and 83 against. Feelings were particularly bitter in the Highlands, especially after stories got out that some Scotsmen had been bribed with English money to accept the agreement. The benefits of the Union did not come quickly to Scotland. It was late in the eighteenth century before cotton, sugar and tobacco imports made Glasgow a prosperous city, and cotton factories turned many west coast villages into busy industrial centres. However, long before that large numbers of Scots had found work in England or made a new life for themselves in the colonies.

George of Hanover

Queen Anne, who signed the Act of Union, was the last of the Stuarts. After suffering from ill-health for most of her life, she died in 1714. All her children had died young, and the Catholic son of James II – also called James – was barred from the throne. Next in line came the Protestant descendants of James I's daughter, Elizabeth. One of her children, Sophia, had

> **SOURCE 5**
>
> Part of the Articles of Union between England and Scotland, 22 July 1706. The Union took effect in the following May. Six years later, in 1713, a motion to dissolve 'this sad and sorrowful union', as Jacobites called it, was narrowly defeated in the House of Lords.

94 Britain United

> **SOURCE 6**
>
> King George I (1714–27).

> **SOURCE 7**
>
> This view of George I comes from the diary of Lord Hervey, who knew the King personally.
>
> In truth he hated the English, looked upon them as King-killers and republicans, grudged them their riches as well as their liberty, thought them overpaid, and said to Lady Sandon one day ... that he was forced to distribute his favour [to] people for being rascals, and pay them not to cut his throat.

married the Elector (ruler) of Hanover in Germany. Their son now became King George I of the new Great Britain.

George was 54 years old and set in his ways. He could not speak English and was only able to communicate with his ministers in Latin or French. He knew very little about the government, laws and customs of his kingdom, yet he seemed in no hurry to learn and spent much of his time in Hanover (**Source 7**). This led to some important changes in the way the country was run.

Both William III and Anne had supervised the government from day to day by meeting regularly with a group of ministers. This group was known as the Cabinet, from the name for a small room. George I was unable to take much part in such discussions and after a while he stopped attending. The Cabinet was then chaired by a leading minister who reported back to the King. This is how the job of 'prime minister' started. The first real prime minister – although he never used the title himself – was Sir Robert Walpole, who was leader of the government from 1721 to 1742. He was particularly skilful at

Crown, Parliament and Union with Scotland

managing Parliament and getting it to do his will.

The King still had an important part to play. His permission was required before a matter could be discussed and nothing could become law unless he agreed to it. However by the time his son, George II, came to rule (1727–60) the prime minister and Cabinet were in control of most of the important affairs of government.

The power of Parliament

Parliament was still dominated by wealthy landowners. MPs did not receive a salary, as they do today. They gave their services free – and considered the time well spent if it ensured that their views were taken into account in the running of the country. The well-to-do had most to lose from bad government. So it was thought fair that their opinions should count for more than those of poorer people. Only about 250,000 men – a very small proportion of the population – had the right to elect MPs to the House of Commons. The voting was not secret. This encouraged candidates to offer bribes to the electors, knowing that they could check up later on the way the votes were cast (**Source 9**).

The reasons why men stood for Parliament often had little to do with politics. They might want to be MPs to keep up a family tradition. They might be keen to make important friends to help them get on in life. Or they might just want to enjoy the busy, exciting life of the capital. Such men were often independent-minded. They might be 'Court' (for the government) on one issue and 'Country' (against) on another. This made it difficult for any monarch to control Parliament. Kings had to choose as their ministers men who had support in the Commons, whether they liked them or not. It is said that William III disliked one of his ministers so much that he never spoke to him!

Members of Parliament were not organised into political parties of the kind we have today. However most MPs called themselves either 'Whigs' or 'Tories' to

SOURCE 8

Sir Robert Walpole, a Norfolk landowner, was Britain's first 'prime minister' – although the title was not an official one until 1905.

SOURCE 9

Bribing the voters at a parliamentary election is described here by a French visitor to England writing in 1747.

The point of most importance in this nation is the election of members to … the Lower House (Commons). The most virtuous [and] wisest … man ought to be preferred, but … the people … sell their votes to those who will give the highest price … During election times, the candidates … sometimes treat three hundred people in a day … Good strong beer will get all you want with the toping (heavy-drinking) countryman; but they that are sober must be won over with money.

QUESTIONS

1. What is a republican? Why did George I suspect the English of being republicans (Source 7)?
2. What effect did the succession of George I have on the power of the monarchy?
3. Many rich and powerful people were against the idea of secret voting in elections. Can you think of any reasons why?
4. MPs acted more independently in the eighteenth century than they do today. Can you explain why?

give some indication of their views. The quarrel between the original Whigs and Tories about whether James II should be allowed to rule was over (see page 80). But many differences and disputes remained.

Tories were loyal, above all, to the monarchy and the Church of England. Some still believed in the Divine Right of Kings (see page 51). Most Tories had never wanted William III as king and were unhappy about his foreign wars. As landowners, they resented paying taxes for the upkeep of the army and navy. The Whigs were glad to see Parliament strengthened at the expense of the Crown. Although they were members of the Church of England, they were inclined to favour Nonconformists and freedom of worship. While most Whigs were landowners, like the Tories, there were also many merchants, bankers and manufacturers in their ranks. They were in favour of expanding trade and gaining more colonies overseas, even at the risk of war (**Source 11**).

The Whigs were in a majority in the House of Commons for most of the time from 1689 to the end of George II's reign (1760). This suited the Hanoverian kings because they knew that the Whig leaders had made sure of their succession to the throne in preference to the Catholic descendants of James II. However Scottish Highlanders and some others were still in favour of restoring the Catholic line of succession to the throne. People with such

SOURCE 10

The House of Commons, painted in 1710.

SOURCE 11

Viscount Bolingbroke was a Tory who tried to get James II's son made king when Queen Anne died. This comes from a book he wrote on the political parties of his day.

We looked upon ... the Revolution of 1688 to be against our true interest ... to have made our people poor and to have weakened Church and State. We supposed the Tory party to be the bulk of the landed interest (landowners and farmers) ... We supposed the Whigs to be so weak a party as to lean for support on the Presbyterians ... the Bank [of England] ... on the Dutch and other allies.

views were known as *Jacobites* – from *Jacobus*, the Latin word for James.

The '15 and '45 rebellions

The Jacobites tried to overthrow the Hanoverian kings twice. In 1715 they planned risings in the north and south-west of England. James Edward Stuart, 'the warming-pan baby' (see page 82), was now known as the Pretender because he claimed to be the rightful king of England. He was due to land in Devon, with the backing of French troops. But many English Jacobites were half-hearted about the rebellion. When the French failed to arrive they were put off completely and took no action.

The one serious rising in 1715 took place in Scotland. Thousands of Scots had become Jacobites simply because of the Union. The clan chiefs formed an army and, in November, fought a drawn battle with royal forces at Sheriff Muir, near Stirling. Most of the clansmen had gone home by the time James, delayed by illness and bad weather, arrived from the Continent to lead the rising. After having himself crowned, he returned to the Continent and settled down in Rome. Meanwhile, hundreds of his supporters, including several lords, were executed for treason.

The second Jacobite rebellion, in 1745, proved more serious. It was led by the Pretender's son, Charles Edward Stuart – known as 'Bonny Prince Charlie'. Charles left Rome without telling his father what he intended to do and went to France to get help. He had chosen a good moment to strike because Britain and France were at war. But bad luck spoilt Jacobite plans. A French fleet, ready to invade England, was destroyed by a storm as it lay in harbour. Despite this setback, Charles sailed to Scotland. In July 1745 he landed on the island of Eriskay in the Outer Hebrides.

Boldly, Charles summoned the clans to meet him. Memories of the '15 rebellion and of the executions afterwards made the Highland chiefs cautious. But they were won over by Charles's charm and courage. Within months, the Highlands had risen in revolt and a clan army took Edinburgh. A government force was massacred at Prestonpans, where a ferocious Highland charge left the battlefield 'littered with heads, legs and arms and mutilated bodies', according to an eyewitness.

Charles proclaimed his father king and marched into England with 5000 men. Crowds watched his fierce, ragged Highlanders go by, but he failed to win much support among English Catholics. By the time he reached Derby, in December, the trap was closing on him. A British army had been brought back from

SOURCE 12

Charles Edward Stuart. He was only 24 when he arrived in Scotland to lead the 1745 Jacobite Rebellion.

the Continent, another had followed him from Scotland, while thousands of citizens were arming themselves to defend London.

The last battle on British soil

Charles turned back at Derby, dodged his enemies and spent a cold winter in the Scottish mountains. His men won another victory over royal forces at Falkirk in January 1746, but their defeat was now only a matter of time. In April, a well-trained army led by the King's son, the Duke of Cumberland, faced the Jacobites on Culloden Moor, near Inverness.

The Highlanders had spent a cold, wet night trying to find Cumberland's camp and launch a surprise attack. They failed and in the morning lined up starving, exhausted and outnumbered. The cannon of the enemy artillery tore into their ranks until they could stand it no longer. They ran forward in a suicidal charge and were massacred by the enemy's musket-fire and massed bayonets (**Source 15**). Few prisoners were taken. The wounded were killed where they lay and innocent onlookers were murdered as well. So ended the last real battle to be fought on British soil. To

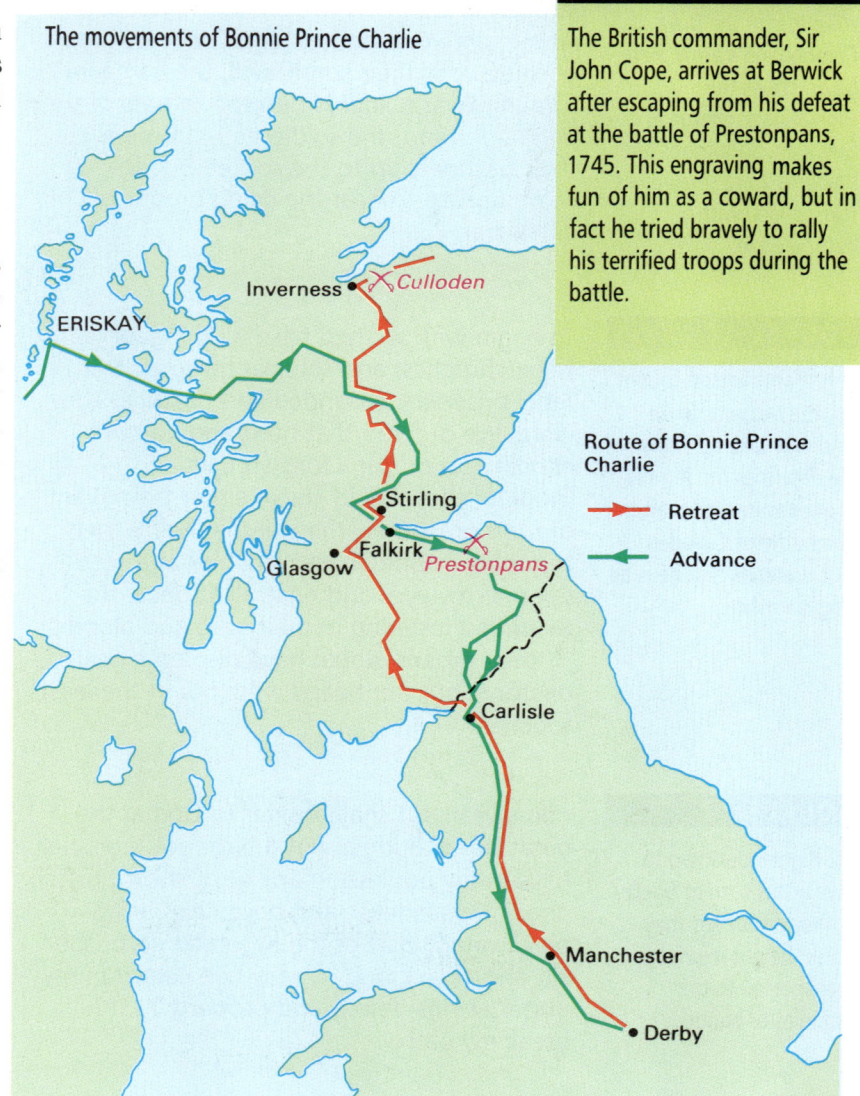

The movements of Bonnie Prince Charlie

Route of Bonnie Prince Charlie
→ Retreat
→ Advance

SOURCE 13

The British commander, Sir John Cope, arrives at Berwick after escaping from his defeat at the battle of Prestonpans, 1745. This engraving makes fun of him as a coward, but in fact he tried bravely to rally his terrified troops during the battle.

Crown, Parliament and Union with Scotland

SOURCE 14

Engraving of the battle of Culloden (1746).

SOURCE 15

Michael Hughes was a volunteer in the Duke of Cumberland's army. Here he describes the Highlanders' charge at Culloden. Spontoons and halberds were small pikes (like spears) with a cutting edge.

It was dreadful to see the enemy's swords circling in the air as they were raised from strokes, and no less to see the officers of the Army, some cutting with their swords, others pushing with their spontoons, the Sergeants running their halberds into the throats of the enemy … [and] the soldiers … ramming their bayonets up to the socket. But still more terrible to hear the dying groans of either party.

SOURCE 16

John Farquharson fought for the Jacobite cause and was taken prisoner. He describes the terrible scenes at Inverness after the battle of Culloden but pretends that he is an English officer.

To begin with we had filled all the gaols, kirks (churches) and ships at Inverness with rebel prisoners, wounded and naked as they were. We ordered that none should have … either meat or drink for two days … [hoping] they would starve either from want of food or clothes, the weather being then very cold … But Oh Heavens! what a scene open to my eyes and nose all at once; the wounded festering in their gore and blood … their groans would have pierced a heart of stone, but our hearts were not in the least touched.

SOURCE 17

All Highlanders had to swear this oath in Gaelic. If they disobeyed they could be put in prison, transported to the colonies or hanged.

I do swear, as I shall answer to God at the great Day of Judgement, I have not, nor shall have in my possession any gun, sword, pistol or arm whatsoever, and never use tartan, plaid, or any part of the Highland garb (the kilt and cloak); and … may I be cursed in my undertakings, family and property … if I break my oath.

QUESTIONS

1. Why did the French side with the Jacobites?
2. Why do you think 'Bonnie Prince Charlie' did not tell his father what he intended to do in 1745?
3. In both 1715 and 1745, why do you think the Jacobite rebels failed to win much support in England?
4. What was the British government trying to achieve when it banned the wearing of the kilt?

this day, Cumberland is known as 'the Butcher' in Scotland.

After the battle, thousands of rebels were tracked down and hanged or transported to the colonies (**Source 16**). Charles escaped to the Continent, after being hunted through the mountains all summer. In the years ahead, the clans were broken up and their chiefs forced to flee abroad. Every effort was made to wipe out the Highland way of life. For a time even bagpipe-playing and wearing the kilt were banned (**Source 17**). When some of the bitterness left by the rebellion had died down, the government raised Highland regiments for the British army, to channel the energies of clansmen. These did heroic service in future wars.

Britain United

Assessment tasks

A Knowledge and understanding

1. **a** What do you think was the main reason why so many Scottish people were against union with England?
   b What was the main reason why, in the end, the Scottish Parliament agreed to the Union?
   c In what ways was Scotland (i) better off, and (ii) worse off, after the Union?

2. What were the chief similarities and differences between (a) Parliament in Tudor times, and (b) Parliament under the early Hanoverians (George I and George II)?

3. Why did the 1715 and 1745 Jacobite rebellions fail? Make a list of (a) reasons which applied to both rebellions, and (b) reasons which applied only to one or the other.

B Interpretations and sources

4. Here are three modern views of the Union of England and Scotland.

   > The Union of 1707 meant that Scotland ... gained ... full partnership in England's markets and colonies. That privilege gave her the opportunity of getting rid at last of her grinding poverty ... [as a result of which] Scotland burst into sudden splendour.
   > (G.M. Trevelyan, 1942)

   > Both countries ... surrendered something ...[The English] gave up exclusive control ...over their political affairs; Scottish commoners (MPs) and sixteen lords ... were free to vote on all matters, even if they were local English or Welsh concerns.
   > (Sir George Clark, 1934)

   > The real trouble with Scotland, since the Union, is that we have not had a say in policy-making. We have always had a small minority in the House of Commons. Even on purely Scottish issues our views could be over-ridden by an English majority ... whose interests were often opposed to ours ... We are neglected ... nothing has made the slightest difference to Scotland's basic problem – unemployment.
   > (Hugh MacDairmid, 1964)

   a What are the points of disagreement between these accounts?
   b Why do you think these disagreements have occurred?

5. From reading Source 7, what do you think George I believed the English thought of him? Was he right?

6. What do the sources in this chapter tell you about:
   a Scottish attitudes towards England and the English?
   b English attitudes towards the Scots?

10 A British Empire

Britain in the early eighteenth century

In the 1720s, a writer named Daniel Defoe toured Britain and wrote reports on the things he saw. In Gloucestershire he stopped to admire Dyrham Park, the home of Sir William Blathwayt. Blathwayt was an important civil servant who dealt with government possessions overseas. These included British colonies in North America and some West Indian islands seized from the Spanish during the seventeenth century. Blathwayt invested money in these countries and, in particular, helped the planters (farmers) in the West Indies whenever he could. They paid him well and he became rich.

Blathwayt turned an old Tudor manor house at Dyrham into a fine mansion. He surrounded it with man-made waterfalls, fountains, hills, lakes and underground streams. The inside of the house was decorated with juniper wood from Jamaica and cedar and walnut from the American colony of Virginia. Many wealthy people Defoe met on his journeys came from fam-

SOURCE 1

Sir William Blathwayt's mansion at Dyrham Park in Gloucestershire. This drawing dates from 1712. Notice the church on the left, where Sir William and his family worshipped, along with their servants and workers.

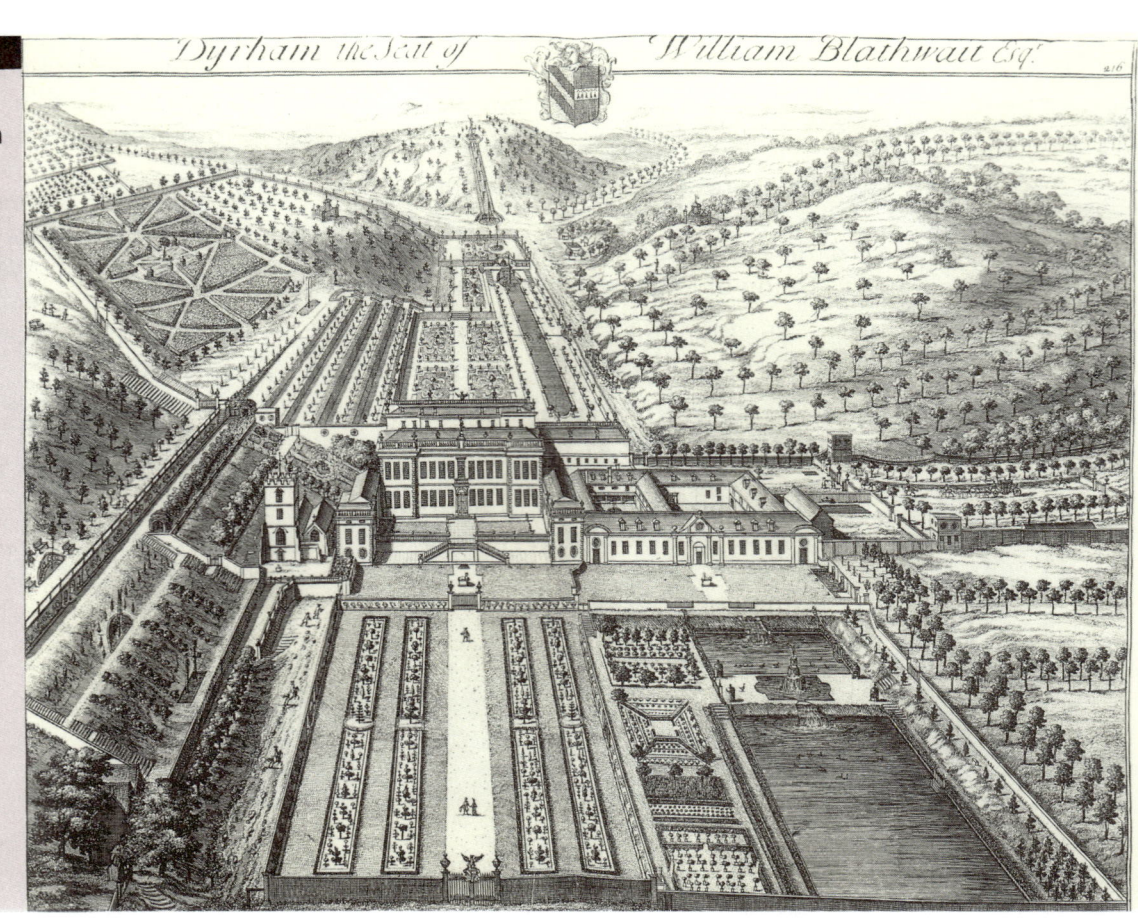

SOURCE 2

This is Gregory King's estimate of the total number of people of each 'rank' in England and Wales, and their income. He included servants in families, so richer people appear to have larger families than poorer ones.

No of families	Ranks, degrees	No. of people per family (household)	Total no. of persons	Yearly income per family
I	**'Increasing the wealth of the kingdom'**			
511,586	Lords, merchants, clergy, farmers, shopkeepers, military officers etc.	5¼	2,675,520	67
II	**'Decreasing the wealth of the kingdom'**			
50,000	Common seaman	3	150,000	20
364,000	Labouring people	3½	1,275,000	15
400,000	Cottagers and paupers	3¼	1,300,000	6.10
35,000	Common soldiers	2	70,000	14
	Vagrants		30,000	
849,000		3¼	2,825,000	10.10
1,360,586	Totals		5,500,520	32

ilies that had done well out of the closing of the monasteries (see Chapter 2). Blathwayt, however, had made money in a new way. His fortune came from an empire which had not existed in 1500.

Estates, degrees and 'the miserable'

How different was eighteenth-century Britain from England in 1500? For a start, of course, it was no longer England, Wales and an independent Scotland but the United Kingdom of Great Britain. Its population was increasing and had probably doubled since 1500. In 1688 Gregory King, a government official, made the first *census* (count) of the population. He checked local registers of births, deaths and taxation and came up with a figure of 5.5 million for England and Wales. We cannot be sure about King's calculations but people at the time thought they were fairly accurate (**Source 2**).

Daniel Defoe graded people into seven classes, starting with those who lived in luxury and ending with 'the miserable that really pinch and suffer want'. These unlucky ones often ended up in the workhouses set up under the Poor Law of 1601 (see page 42) (**Source 3**). People still talked of being born into an 'estate' or 'degree', as in Tudor times, although it was always possible to move from one to another. Blathwayt, for example, had not been born into a rich family but had moved up in society.

There was a great deal of snobbery in this period. Most people looked down upon somebody else. A gentleman despised a merchant; a physician thought he was better than a surgeon. The housekeeper of a noble family would look down on the cook, and the cook on the gardener. The worst snobs were noblemen and women. 'It is monstrous to be told that you

SOURCE 3

These rules of an eighteenth-century workhouse come from Wimbledon in Surrey.

Such of the poor as shall be guilty of ... indecent and abusive language or mocking and scoffing ... shall be debarred (lose) their next meal ... Each poor person [admitted] shall deliver up all their goods for the benefit of the parish and they are not to have any box, drawer, or other receptacle under lock and key ... but each of them receive from the matron a proper box ... for holding their linen and clothes ... All poor persons are to perform to the utmost of their power their work.

have a heart as sinful as the common wretches that crawl the earth', said the Duchess of Buckingham when a clergyman told her all people were sinners in the eyes of God!

One big change since 1500 was in religion. In the early sixteenth century everyone had belonged to the Catholic Church. By 1700 people were split into three groups – Anglicans (Church of England), Catholics and Nonconformists. The Church of England was dominant. It was the state Church and those in positions of power in local and national life belonged to it. In country areas the owners of large estates, known as squires, usually took a close interest in their local church and appointed the parish priest (**Source 4**). Even bishops often owed their position to being related to a noble family or having once worked in a nobleman's household as a chaplain or tutor.

Country clergymen were often landowners themselves. Some were not very hardworking and preferred to pay an assistant, called a curate, to take most of the services and look after the parishioners. Curates and the vicars of poor parishes found it hard to make ends meet. Defoe met one who delivered coal in his spare time to earn a little extra money!

Anglican clergymen disliked Nonconformist ministers, who were now free to hold services in their own meeting houses. Most Nonconformists lived in towns, where the influence of the Church of England was not so strong. They were

SOURCE 4

Joseph Addison (1672–1719), a writer, invented a character called Sir Roger de Coverley, who was meant to be a typical squire of the time. Sir Roger gave much time and energy to his parish church.

My friend, Sir Roger ... told me that at his coming to his estate he found the parishioners very irregular; and in order to make them kneel and join in the responses, he gave everyone of them a hassock (kneeling cushion) and a Common-Prayer book; at the same time employing ... a singing master to teach them the tunes of the Psalms. As Sir Roger is landlord to the whole congregation, he keeps them in very good order, and suffers nobody to sleep [in the church] apart from himself.

SOURCE 5

Nonconformist meeting houses were very different from churches. This is a Quaker meeting house at Jordans in Buckinghamshire, built in 1688. 'Quaker' was a nickname for the Society of Friends, founded by George Fox (1624–91), because people said they quaked (trembled) before God. Instead of having set orders of services, they preferred to rely on inspiration from God.

QUESTIONS

1. How might workhouse rules (Source 3) have taken away people's self-respect?
2. Why do you think gentlemen considered themselves superior to merchants, and cooks looked down upon gardeners?
3. Why did the congregation do what they were told by Sir Roger (Source 4)?
4. What does the Jordans meeting house (Source 5) tell you about the attitudes of Quakers towards their religion?

SOURCE 6

An English family taking tea in 1720. Tea was still an expensive luxury, so the lady of the house (seated left) is measuring it out from a tea-caddy normally kept in a locked wooden box.

still banned from the universities, so they ran their own schools and academies. Daniel Defoe was a Nonconformist who had been educated at what was called a 'dissenting academy'. Catholics were still very unpopular and distrusted. Their priests were no longer persecuted but there were many laws against them.

The 'new look' North

Daniel Defoe travelled through a country that was much more like our own than the one described by Polydore Vergil (see Chapter 1). There were newspapers and banks, both unknown in 1500, and coffee-houses where men could meet to discuss business and politics and catch up with the latest gossip. Both coffee and tea had become fashionable since the 1650s, when regular supplies started to be shipped from India, China and the Middle East.

People's living standards had risen since 1500. In the South, many towns were doing well out of foreign trade and the country-side was dotted with large mansions and new-style gardens like Dyrham Park

SOURCE 7

By the eighteenth century the gardens of great houses were being designed to look like pretty country scenes, with man-made hills, woods and lakes. The most famous designer of such 'landscape gardens' was Lancelot 'Capability' Brown, so called because he remarked to one nobleman about his estate: 'I see great capability of improvement here'. This is part of the landscape garden Brown designed at Blenheim Palace in Oxfordshire.

(**Source 7**). The North was still poorer than the South. There, as one man told Defoe, ordinary folk usually went barefoot. But it was in the North, with its growing industries, that some of the most important changes were taking place.

Yorkshire had become the main centre of the woollen cloth industry. When Defoe visited the area on one of his tours, in 1724, he found it to be one of the most prosperous and heavily populated parts of England (**Source 8**). He also remarked that the Yorkshire towns of Sheffield and Barnsley were dark and grimy with the smoke of forges and iron-workshops.

Iron manufacturing and industries such as brewing and brick-making were using increasing amounts of coal. Much of this was produced in north-eastern England, around the rivers Tyne and Wear, and carried away by sea. Between 1700 and 1750, coal output in Britain doubled, from 2½ million tonnes to just under 5 million. This increase was achieved by miners using only hand tools.

Defoe saw busy industrial towns and villages eating into the countryside in many parts of the North. Some, including Liverpool and Manchester, had hardly existed in Tudor times. Liverpool, growing rich from its cotton and sugar trade with America, was, said Defoe, 'one of the wonders of the world', with fine new buildings, streets and squares. Manchester, where American cotton was turned into cloth in hundreds of workshops, was, he claimed, 'the greatest mere village in England'. But while mine-owners, merchants and businessmen were doing well, most ordinary workers were paid a pittance and struggled to make ends meet (**Source 9**).

London life

London, with a population of well over half a million in 1700, was ten times larger than any other city in Britain. 'The whole kingdom as well as the people ... are employed to furnish the best of everything for London', reported Defoe. Cattle and oats from Scotland, grain from the Midlands, fruit and hops from Kent and Worcestershire, geese and chickens from Surrey and Sussex, turkeys from East Anglia and a thousand other commodities poured into the capital. When asked why Reading in Berkshire was prosperous,

SOURCE 8

Here is part of Daniel Defoe's description of the cloth industry in the west of Yorkshire (1724). Carding involved disentangling the fibres of the wool to prepare it for spinning.

We saw the houses full of lusty (strong) fellows, some at the dye-vat, some at the loom, others dressing the cloths; the women and children carding or spinning; all employed, from the youngest to the oldest; [there was hardly a child] above four years old but its hands were sufficient for its own support. Not a beggar to be seen, nor an idle person ... Some of these remote parts of the North are the most populous (populated) places of Great Britain [apart from] London and its neighbourhood.

SOURCE 9

Here Defoe describes a meeting with a woman in the Peak District of Derbyshire. He thought it would 'show the discontented rich how to value their own good fortune'.

Can I come in and see your house, dame? said one of our company ... We went in. There was a large hollow cave, which the poor people, by two curtains hanged across, had parted into two rooms. On one side was a chimney ... The habitation was poor ... [but] clean and neat ... There were shelves with earthen ware, and some pewter and brass. There was bacon hanging up in the chimney ... and a sow and pigs running about at the door ... and a little lean cow and a little piece of ground was growing with good barley ... I asked the poor woman what trade her husband was? She said he worked in the lead mines.

QUESTIONS

1 In what ways was the cloth-making described by Defoe (Source 8) organised differently from today?

2 Why was coal usually transported on water in this period?

3 Why was Liverpool a more suitable port for receiving goods from America than London?

4 Can you think of any reason Defoe might have had for calling Manchester 'the greatest mere village' rather than a town?

SOURCE 10

A London street scene in the eighteenth century – the Lord Mayor's Show.

Defoe wrote simply, 'its chief trade is by water navigation to and from London'.

It was not only food that came to the capital. 'The butcher, the baker, the candlestick-maker' and many other craftsmen settled in London. Poor people needed basic necessities. The rich demanded fine houses, elegant coaches, fashionable clothes, jewels, wigs and countless other luxuries. They employed barbers to cut their hair, dancing masters to prepare them for the ball and hundreds of servants in their houses, stables and gardens. There was hardly a craft or trade not represented in London, from goldsmiths, tailors and cabinet-makers to the shipwrights, dockers and bargemen who inhabited the narrow streets and alleys by the waterside.

Life was hard for the poorer people of London. They worked long hours for low pay and lived in dirty, overcrowded slums which bred all kinds of disease. Many got drunk to forget the cares of the world, and vice and crime flourished – despite cruel punishments. Men, women and children were hanged for picking pockets and similar petty offences. Such executions were regarded as great public entertainment (**Source 11**). Crowds followed the procession of condemned criminals from Newgate Gaol to the gallows at Tyburn (along present-day Oxford Street). People were also entertained by the sufferings of animals, especially cock-fighting (**Source 12**) and baiting bulls and bears with dogs.

SOURCE 11

A public execution. This occurred in Edinburgh in the mid-eighteenth century. The condemned man was a murderer named Norman Ross. Notice that his right hand was cut off first. Can you think of a reason for this?

Britain in the early eighteenth century **107**

The largest towns outside London were Norwich, centre of the East Anglian cloth industry, and Bristol, expanding rapidly on the profits of trade with North America. In Scotland, Glasgow was also prospering on American trade and Edinburgh remained the centre of the country's social life. But none of these could approach the size and variety of London. Some cities, such as Salisbury and Lincoln, were known for their cathedrals. Oxford and Cambridge were famous as university towns. And spa towns, where people bathed for the good of their health in hot springs and wells, were becoming fashionable pleasure resorts for the rich. The most popular spa was Bath, with its newly-built terraces of elegant houses, paved streets and fine public buildings.

Colonies and trade

Three cities Defoe admired – Liverpool, Manchester and Bristol – were growing rich because of world-wide trade. This had been unknown in 1500. Since the great voyages of discovery, made mainly by the Spanish and Portuguese in the fifteenth and early sixteenth centuries, the riches of the world had been opened up to Europeans. English, Dutch, Spanish and French merchants competed for trade, founding colonies in the Americas and setting up trading stations in the East. Little thought was given to the wishes of the people who were colonised (**Source 13**).

Competition for colonies and trade led to wars on sea and land. The British fleet did well in battles against the French and Dutch, and by Defoe's time British merchant ships could sail the world's oceans without much fear of attack. In 1700 the English had twelve colonies in North America (a thirteenth was added in 1733), valuable trading bases in India and rich possessions in the West Indies. The Spanish ruled most of South America. The French were in parts of North America and, with the Dutch, struggling to get Indian trade away from the English.

In 1713 the British signed the Treaty of Utrecht with France and Spain to end a long war in which they had won great victories. They gained the islands of Gibraltar and Minorca in the Mediterranean and most of Canada. Also, for the first time Spain let the British trade with Spanish America. In particular, they granted Britain the sole right to carry African slaves to Spanish colonies in the New World. Previously many European countries had taken part in the slave trade, although it was an English sailor, Sir John Hawkins, who started it in 1562.

British ships carried slaves as part of a round trip of voyages known as the Triangle of Trade (see diagram). British-made goods, such as cloth, guns, beads, pots and pans, were shipped to West Africa. These were exchanged for black

SOURCE 12

This account of cock-fighting in London was written by a Swiss visitor, Cesar de Saussure, in the 1720s. The cocks always fought to the death.

The animals used are ... large but short-legged birds ... very ugly to look at ... The stage on which they fight is round and small. One of the cocks is released and struts about proudly for a few seconds. He is then caught up, and his enemy appears. When the bets are made ... they immediately rush at each other and fight furiously ... The noise is terrible, and it is impossible to hear yourself speak unless you shout ... Cocks will sometimes fight a whole hour before one or the other is victorious; at other times one may get killed at once.

SOURCE 13

This comes from Jonathan Swift's famous book, *Gulliver's Travels*, 1726. It tells the fantastic story of a sailor shipwrecked on an island, Lilliput, where the people are tiny, and in Brobdingnag, where they are all 'tall as steeples'.

A crew of pirates are driven by a storm they know not whither; at length a boy discovers land from the topmast; they go on shore to rob and plunder; they see a harmless people, are entertained with kindness; they give the country a new name; they take possession of it for their king; ... they murder two or three dozen of the natives ... ships are sent at the first opportunity; the natives driven out and destroyed; their princes tortured to discover gold ... [this is] a modern colony

The British 'Triangular Trade'

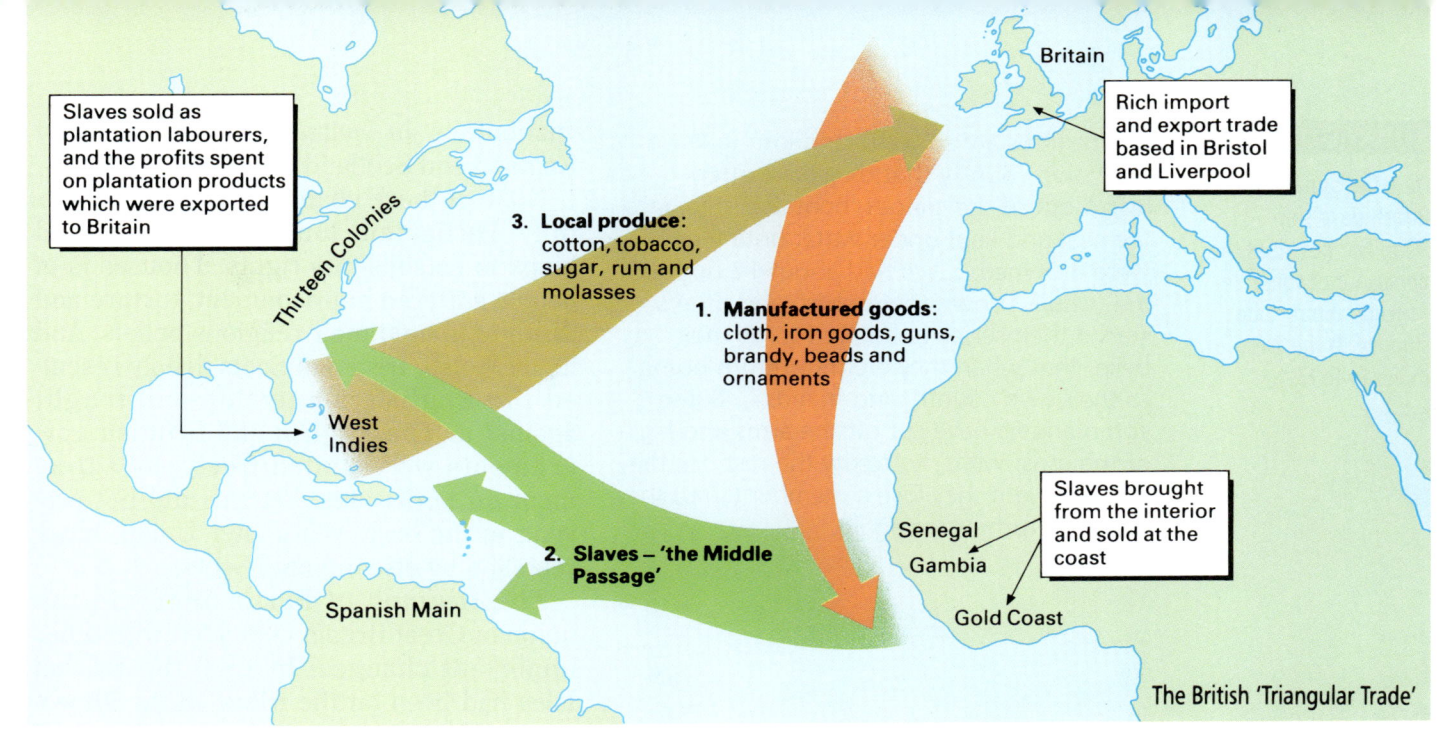

- Slaves sold as plantation labourers, and the profits spent on plantation products which were exported to Britain
- Rich import and export trade based in Bristol and Liverpool
- Slaves brought from the interior and sold at the coast

1. **Manufactured goods:** cloth, iron goods, guns, brandy, beads and ornaments
2. **Slaves – 'the Middle Passage'**
3. **Local produce:** cotton, tobacco, sugar, rum and molasses

slaves who were tied up and packed shoulder to shoulder on the ships' decks. Many slaves killed themselves (**Source 16**). Many more died from disease on the long voyage across the Atlantic. Those who survived were sold to planters who put them to work growing rice, sugar, tobacco and cotton. Profits from the sale of slaves were used to buy cargoes of these crops for the home voyage – the third stage of a deadly Triangle which brought riches to the merchants of Liverpool and Bristol.

Britain and the New World

This book has described changes and events which still affect our lives today. We have seen how Parliament, the occasional adviser of the king in 1500, became his master after the 1688 Revolution. We have seen how religious persecution gave way to freedom of worship. We have also seen how the people of the British Isles came to be bound together more tightly, by the Welsh Acts of Union, the English

SOURCE 14

Surat, in India – a fortified trading post of the East India Company. Founded in London in 1600, the Company originally traded with the Moluccas (now Indonesia) in the East Indies, until driven out by the Dutch in 1623. This explains its name.

Britain in the early eighteenth century **109**

SOURCE 16

Here the captain of a British slave-ship, *Hannibal*, describes the behaviour of some Africans about to be shipped to the West Indies in 1693-4.

The negroes are so wilful and loth to leave their own country that they have often leap'd out of the canoes, boat and ship, into the sea, and kept under water until they were drowned ... We had about 12 negroes did wilfully drown themselves, and others starv'd themselves to death; for 'tis their belief that when they die they return home to their own country and friends ... Some commanders have cut off the arms and legs of the most wilful, to terrify the rest, for they believe that if they lose a member (limb) they cannot return home again.

'plantations' in Ireland and the joining of England and Scotland in 1707.

None of these changes happened peacefully. Parliament fought and dethroned kings to establish its rights. Thousands of people suffered imprisonment, torture and death to uphold their religious beliefs. And many Welsh, Irish and Scots deeply resented the English connection and fought against it. The English and Scottish governments were united freely, by agreement on both sides. Yet this did not prevent, in the early years after Union, bitter rebellion by discontented Scots.

The triumph of Parliament and the union of Great Britain coincided with other important changes. In 1500 the British Isles had been on the fringe of the known world. The vastness of the Americas had yet to be discovered by Europeans. By the eighteenth century the New World had been opened up to the peoples of Europe. Britain was in a fine position geographically, set like a spider in a web of trade routes. A global empire was in the making – an empire governed by the United Kingdom of Great Britain.

The British Empire in 1750

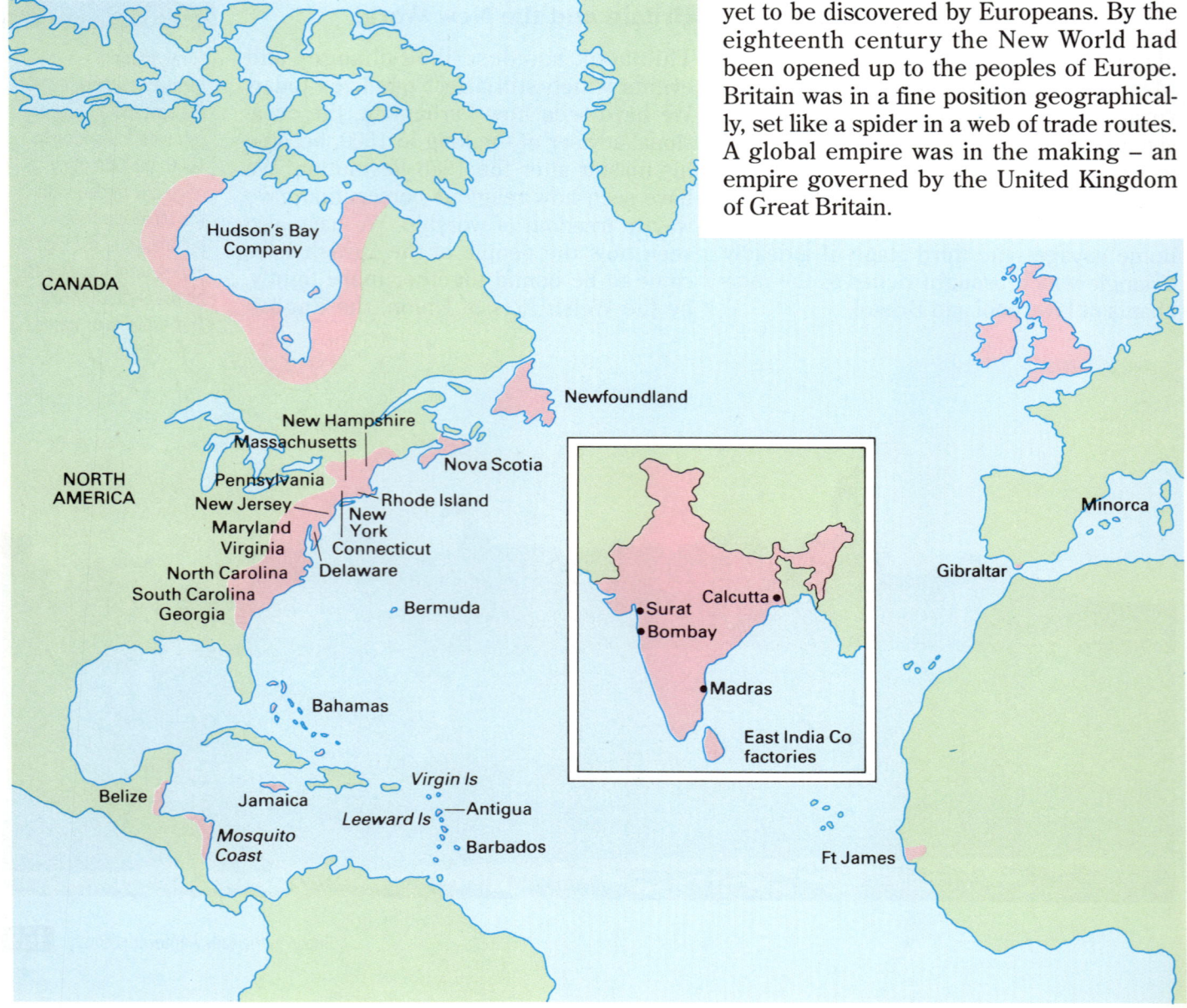

Assessment tasks

A Knowledge and understanding

1 What were the main differences between England in 1500 and Britain in 1750? List them under three headings, as follows: *political* (to do with those who have power and the way decisions are made); *social* (affecting the day to day lives of the people), and *religious* (to do with beliefs, the Churches and ways of worshipping).

2 Can you explain how the growth of British colonies and trade, (a) made life better for some people, and (b) made it worse for others? Give examples where you can.

3 Outline some of the main *regional* differences in the life and work of British people in the early eighteenth century. For example, you might compare the North with the South, East Anglia with Wales and the west coast.

B Interpretations and sources

4 Here are two modern views of the African slave trade.

> Although white men came to take such a large part in the African slave trade it is fair to remember that they did not begin in it ... The Africans themselves used to make slaves of the tribes they defeated ... So when the Europeans first came to Nigeria they came to a country where every powerful chief had as many slaves as he could afford.
> (S.S. Moody, 1963)

> In the sixteenth century, Central Africa was a territory of peace and happy civilisation. The tribal wars from which European pirates claimed to deliver the people were mere sham-fights; it was a great battle when half a dozen men were killed. It was on [these people] that the slave trade fell. Tribal life was broken up and millions of Africans ... let loose upon each other ... Tribes had to supply slaves or be sold as slaves themselves. Violence ... became necessary for survival.
> (C.L.R. James, 1938)

a What are the main points of disagreement between these two accounts, and how might such differences have arisen?
b Which account do you find the most convincing, and why?

5 Look carefully at Source 2.
a How useful do you find Gregory King's figures as a source of information about the English people at that time (1688)?
b Can you think of his reason for making these calculations? Why would his figures have interested the government?

6 What do the sources taken from the works of early eighteenth-century writers (Defoe, Addison and Swift) add to your understanding of the history of this period?

Index

Topics in the National Curriculum Orders are in bold type.
Page numbers in *italics* refer to illustrations.

Acts of Union: Wales 23, 25, 26
Scotland 92–4
Anglicans – see **Church of England**
Anne, Queen 83, 84, 85, *92*, 94, 95
Anne Boleyn 18-9, *24*
Anne of Cleves 24
Architecture 39-40, 71-2, 102, 105
Armada, Spanish 34-6
Arthur, Prince 16, 17, 18
Arts 45-6, 72-3
Aske, Robert 22-3

Babington, Anthony 33, 34, 37
Bank of England 85
Bastwicke, John 54, 59
Bath 108
Bible, English 20-*1, 50*
Bill of Rights 84, 85
Blathwayt, Sir William *102*-3
'Bonnie Prince Charlie' – see Charles Edward Stuart
Bosworth, battle of 16
Boyne, battle of the 88
Bristol 10, 108, 109
Buckingham, Duke of 50, 53, 54
Burghley, Lord 40, 41
Burton, Henry 54, 59

Cabinet government 95
Calvin, John *30*
Cambridge 44, 108
Campeggio, Cardinal 19
Campion, Edmund 31
Canada 108
Catherine of Aragon 18-9, *24*, 28
Catherine Howard 24
Catherine Parr 24
Catholics 17, 20, 27, 28, 30, 31, 51, 52, 53, 80-8, 97-8, 104-5
Charles I *53*-8, 61-6
Charles II 66, *68*, 70, 80
Charles V, Emperor 17, 19
Charles Edward Stuart 98-100
Church, the – see **Religion**
Church of England 20, 30, 104
Circulation of the blood 77-8
Civil War, the English 58, 60-5
Clement VII, Pope 18, 19
Coalmining 9, 10, 106

Coffee houses 105
Colonies, British 102, 108, *110*
Commonwealth – see **Interregnum**
Court, the 9, *12*, 13
Cranmer, Thomas 19, 27, 28
Cromwell, Oliver *63*-7, 69
Cromwell, Richard 67-8
Cromwell, Thomas *20*, 21, 22
Crown – see **Monarchy**
Culloden Moor, battle of 99-*100*
Cumberland, Duke of 99, 100

Daily Courant 85
Declaration of Indulgence 82, 83
Defoe, Daniel 102, 103, 105, 106
Derby 98, 99
'Divine Right' – see **Monarchy**
Dryden, John 72, 73
Dudley, Robert Earl of Leicester 31, 41, 44
Dunbar, battle of 66

East India Company *109*
Edgehill, battle of *61*-2
Edinburgh 56, 98, 108
Education 42-4
Edward VI 23, 27, *28*
Elections 13, 96
'Eleven Years Tyranny' 54
Eliot, Sir John 54
Elizabeth I 14, 19, 29-*36*, *38*, 40-1, 45-6
Enclosure 7, 15
Enniskellen 87
Essex, Earl of 47

Fairfax, Thomas 63
Farming 6-7
Fawkes, Guy 51
Felton, John 54
Fire of London 70-1
Flodden, battle of 17

Galileo 74
George I 95
Gibraltar 108
Glasgow 93, 94, 108
Glencoe Massacre 86-*7*
'Glorious Revolution' 80, 83-5, 86, 87
Gloucester 62
Grand Remonstrance 58
Gunpowder Plot *51*-2
Gwynne, Nell 72

Hampden, John 54
Harvey, William 77-8
Henry VII 6, 12, 14, *16*-8
Henry VIII 14, 17-25
Hooke, Robert 72, *73*
Houses 39-40, *102, 105*

Interregnum, the 66-8
Ireland 46-7, 48, *57*, 63, 66, *87*-9, 90-1
Iron industry 106

Jacobites 98-*100*
Jamaica 67
James I 47, *49*-53
James II 80-4, 87-8
James Edward Stuart 98
Jane Seymour 23, *24*
Jeffreys, Judge 81-2
Jesuits – see Society of Jesus

Killiecrankie, battle of 86
King, Gregory 103

Latimer, Hugh 29
Laud, Archbishop 54, *55*, 56, 57
Lee, Bishop Rowland 24-5
Leo X, Pope 17
Leslie, David 63
Levellers, the 64
Limerick, Treaty of 88-9
Liverpool 106, 108, 109
London 9, *10-11*, 45, 68, 70-*1*, 106-8
Londonderry 87, *88*, 90-*1*
Luther, Martin 17-8

Manchester 106, 108
Marston Moor, battle of 63, 69
Mary I (Tudor) 18, *28*-9
Mary II 80, 84, 85
Mary Beatrice, Queen 82-*3*
Mary Rose, The 23
Mary Stuart (Queen of Scots) 30, 31, *33-34*, 37
Medicine 76
Microscope 72, *73*
Milton, John 72, *73*
Minorca 108
Monarchy, nature of 12-4, 51, 84-5, 95-6
relations with the Church 17-23, 27-31, 50-1, 54, 56, 80, 82, 85
relations with Parliament 13-4, 19-20, 22, 31-3, 51, 53-8, 68, 80, 84-5, 96-7, 109
relations with the people 22-3, 36, 38, 40-1,
49-50, 60-1, 82-3
Monasteries, dissolution of 21-2, 41
Monck, General George 68
Monmouth, Duke of 80-1
Monopolies 41, 53
Mountjoy, Earl of 47

Nantwich, battle of 63
Naseby, battle of 64
National Covenant 56
Newcastle 10
New Model Army 63-4, 65, 66, 67, 68, 92
Newspapers 85
Newton, Isaac 74, *75*
Nonconformists 82, 85, 97, 104, 105
Norfolk, Duke of 22-3
North, the 9-10, 105-6
Northumberland, Earls of 9, 10
Norwich 10, 41, 108

Open fields – see farming
Oxford 43, 44, 108

Parliament 13-4, 19-20, 22, 31-3, 51, 53-8, 68, 80, 84-5, 96-7, 109
Pepys, Samuel *70*, 71, 72
Petition of Right 53, 54
Philip II, King of Spain 28, *29*, 33-4, 47
Pilgrimage of Grace 22-3
Plague, the 70, 75, 76
Poor Laws 41-*2*, 43
Pope, the *17*-8, 19, 20, 31, 74
Population 10, 103
Prayer Book 27, 28, 29, 30, 56
Presbyterians 30, 50
Prestonpans, battle of 98, *99*
Pride, Colonel 65
Privy Council 13
Protestants – see **Religion**
Prynne, William 54, 59
Puritans 30, 50
Pym, John 56, 58

Reformation, the 19-23
Regional differences 6, 9-10, 105-6
Religion 17-23, 27-31, 50, 54-6, 63, 64, 76, 80, 85, 87-8, 104, 109
Richard III 12, 16, 46
Ridley, Nicholas 29
Roman Catholics – see **Catholics**

Roses, Wars of 12, 16
Royal Society 72, 75, 79
Rupert, Prince 61-2, 63, 64, 72

St Paul's Cathedral *11*, 71
Schools – see Education
'Scientific Revolution', 72, 73, 74-78
Scotland 17, 49, 56, 64, 65, 66, 86, 92-4, 97-100, 101, 110
Sedgemoor, battle of 81
Shakespeare, William 41, 45-6
Sheriff Muir, battle of 98
Ship Money 54
Sidney, Sir Henry 25
Slave trade 108-9, 110, 111
Social 'classes' 7-10, 102-4, 107
Society of Jesus 31
Spain 33-4
Statute of Artificers 41
Strafford, Earl – see Wentworth, Thomas

Tea 105
Telescope 74
Theatre, the 45-6, 72
Tories 80, 96-7
Towns 10-2, 106-8
Trade 108-9

United Kingdom, unification of 25, 49, 92-4, 101, 109-10
Universities 43-4
Utrecht, Treaty of 108

Vergil, Polydore 6

Wales 16, 23-5, 26
Walpole, Sir Robert 95-*6*
Wentworth, Peter 32, 33
Wentworth, Thomas (Earl of Strafford) 54, *56*, 57
Whigs 80, 96-7
Wight, Isle of *23*, 64
William III 80, *81*, 84-9, 90-*1*, 95, 96
Wolsey, Archbishop 17, 18, *19*
Woollen cloth industry 9, 106
Worcester, battle of 66
Workhouses 42, 103
Wren, Christopher 71-2

Yeomen 8, 40
York 10